WILLIAM BLAKE
AT
THE HUNTINGTON

WILLIAM BLAKE
AT
THE HUNTINGTON

An Introduction to the
William Blake Collection
in The Henry E. Huntington Library
and Art Gallery
San Marino, California

Robert N. Essick

Harry N. Abrams, Inc., Publishers
in association with The Henry E. Huntington Library
and Art Gallery

Editors: Diana Murphy, Mark Greenberg

Library of Congress Cataloging-in-Publication Data

Henry E. Huntington Library and Art Gallery.
    William Blake at the Huntington: an introduction to the William
Blake Collection in the Henry E. Huntington Library and Art Gallery,
San Marino, California / Robert N. Essick.
        p.   cm.
    Includes bibliographical references and index.
    "In association with the Henry E. Huntington Library and Art
Gallery."
    ISBN 0–8109–2589–3
    1. Blake, William, 1757–1827—Catalogs.   2. Art—California—San
Marino—Catalogs.   3. Henry E. Huntington Library and Art Gallery—
Catalogs.   I. Essick, Robert N.   II. Title.
N6797.B57A4   1994
760'.092—dc20   94–4370

Front cover: *Satan, Sin, and Death: Satan Comes to the Gates of Hell.*
c. 1806 (Illus. 54)
Back cover: *Comus, Disguised as a Rustic, Addresses the Lady in the Wood,* one of
eight illustrations to John Milton's *Comus.* Fall 1801–1802 (Illus. 30)
Title page: *Satan Watching the Endearments of Adam and Eve,* one of twelve
illustrations to John Milton's *Paradise Lost.* 1807 (Illus. 46)

CONTENTS

FOREWORD

The occasion for this publication, devoted to the work of the great British poet and artist William Blake, is the seventy-fifth anniversary of the founding in 1919 of The Henry E. Huntington Library and Art Gallery. The Huntington collection of Blake—manuscripts, illustrated books, illuminated volumes, individual works of art—is extensive and, as Robert Essick points out in his essay, one of the finest in the world. Although well known to scholars, the works in the collection have not been available to a wide audience. The present selection will rectify that situation. As a pictorial introduction to Blake, it is the first publication to highlight the unique or rare pieces at the Huntington and to reproduce them in color.

The book would not have been possible without Robert N. Essick. An internationally recognized expert on Blake, Mr. Essick published in 1985 a scholarly catalogue of the Huntington's entire collection of the artist. His introductory essay to the volume places Blake in a historical context that emphasizes his ties to the art and thought of the period, but also gives a sense of Blake as a visionary. The commentaries on the works themselves offer insights into the poet's philosophical and artistic concerns.

I wish to take this opportunity to thank Robert Essick for his ongoing commitment to the Huntington. Over the years, he has generously contributed his time and support to various activities and programs. His dedication to the educational and cultural aims of the institution has repeatedly manifested itself. The following work is just the most recent example of his involvement.

While all of us at the Huntington are indebted to Mr. Essick for the realization of this book, he wishes to acknowledge in particular: Shelley Bennett, Curator of British and Continental Art, for her enthusiasm for the publication and for her curatorial guidance; Jacqueline Dugas, for assistance with the volume's preparation; Deidre Cantrell and Edward Seffel, for computer help; and Robert Schlosser, for photography. His greatest debt, however, is to Jenijoy La Belle.

EDWARD J. NYGREN
DIRECTOR OF THE ART COLLECTIONS

INTRODUCTION

William Blake has become one of the English-speaking world's most renowned poets and artists. His writings are taught frequently in schools and studied intensively by scholars. During the last fifteen years, exhibitions of his art in London, Toronto, New Haven, and Tokyo have attracted large and ardent crowds. His brief lyric "The Tyger" may be the most anthologized poem in the language. But such fame was not always Blake's lot. In his own lifetime, his works were hardly known beyond a small band of patrons and connoisseurs. Throughout the last century and the early decades of our own, Blake's writings were kept alive by a handful of enthusiasts, including the poets D. G. Rossetti and W. B. Yeats, who admired the energy and complexity of his works. An equally small number of collectors treasured Blake's prints and drawings. Among this latter group was the great American bibliophile Henry E. Huntington. Shortly before he established The Henry E. Huntington Library and Art Gallery in 1919, he began to acquire for the new institution some of Blake's rarest and finest works, both visual and verbal. By the time of his death in 1927, Huntington had created one of the world's great Blake collections, particularly notable for the way it represents the full range of Blake's endeavors in many media. Indeed, a survey of the collection provides a good general introduction to Blake, and it is also true that the following brief introduction to Blake's life and works can serve as a guide to the Huntington collection.

Born on November 28, 1757, Blake was the third son of a London hosier. The city of his birth, where he lived for all but three years of his life, and the social class of shopkeepers in which he was raised had profound influences on the course of Blake's life. He showed talent at drawing while still a child and hoped to become an artist. But the family purse could not support such high ambitions, and Blake was apprenticed at the age of fourteen to the engraver James Basire. Like most members of his craft, Basire was engaged principally in reproducing works by other artists or making straightforward pictures of objects to illustrate books and periodicals. Such work placed the master and his apprentices in close proximity to the artistic and intellectual life of London, but not at its center. This and other types of marginality, cultural and economic, haunted Blake throughout his career.

Blake's seven years of training as an etcher-engraver gave the young man more than a profession. His master's shop practiced an old-fashioned, linear graphic technique. This style must have suited Blake's life-long interest in early printmaking and contributed to one of his central aesthetic concepts expressed in his later writings: the artistic, and even philosophical, superiority of line to color. Basire was engraver to the Society of Antiquaries and executed many illustrations for publications by the Royal Society. These activities brought Blake into contact with antiquarian studies, classical and British, and the most recent advances in the sciences. The clash between the antique and the contemporary and attempts to reconcile the two lie behind much in Blake's later life in the arts. What we find "visionary" or even strikingly modern in Blake's pictures and poems is frequently a product of his attempt to recover what he believed to be ancient styles and images.

After his release from apprenticeship in 1779, Blake began to establish himself as an engraver. Reproducing illustrations for booksellers, and occasionally separate prints sold individually, became Blake's occupation and remained so for many years. In the summer of 1782 he married Catherine Boucher, the daughter of a market gardener. She was Blake's helpmate to the end of his days and almost certainly a far greater influence on his life and work than is indicated by the few extant records about her. Within the next two years, Blake began a print selling and publishing business with James Parker, another former apprentice of Basire's, but the partnership appears to have been short-lived and produced only two plates. While these essentially commercial activities proceeded along conventional lines for a man of Blake's training and status as an urban artisan, his talents led him in more ambitious directions.

Blake had scribbled verses, some of considerable quality, since his childhood. A group of friends sponsored the publication of a slim volume of these poems in 1783, entitled *Poetical Sketches.* Although the collection is now seen as the seminal work of a great poet, it left no mark on the literary landscape of the 1780s. Fewer than twenty-five copies have survived; two are in the Huntington Library. These halting steps toward a career in writing were matched by Blake's desire to become an artist. He enrolled as a student in the Royal Academy schools in the fall of 1779 and exhibited watercolors in its annual show the next year. At the Academy, Blake was trained in drawing from life and from casts of classical sculptures. Of equal importance in the formation of Blake's pictorial art was his friendship with two young men also just beginning their careers, Thomas Stothard and John Flaxman.

The 1780s was a time of artistic as much as political turmoil. History painting, which took its heroic subjects from real events or imaginative literature, remained at the top of the hierarchy of genres; but other forms, including portraiture and landscape, were at least as popular. Young artists like Blake and his friends had several different styles in which to try their talents. Chief among these were the Rococo, a highly decorative mode inherited from the earlier years of the eighteenth century, and the Neoclassical, a self-consciously historical style of linear abstraction based on Greek and Roman art. Stothard became a successful artist and book illustrator in a genteel version of Rococo, often allied with the picturesque, while Flaxman became England's greatest Neoclassical sculptor. Blake's art in the 1780s shows clear Neoclassical tendencies that go hand-in-hand with his strong preference for the linear over the painterly. The development of Blake's later and most characteristic styles owes much to the contentious varieties of taste and technique that produced what we now call Romanticism.

By the final years of the decade, Blake must have felt some disappointment, given his high ambitions as an artist, engraver, and poet. There is no evidence that the institutions of exhibition and publication were receptive to his efforts. He managed to have only one further poem printed by conventional means, *The French Revolution* of 1791, but it may never have been published. The single extant copy, now in the Huntington Library, may only be a set of page proofs. The great printsellers John and Josiah Boydell hired Blake, in 1788, to execute one large separate plate after a painting by William Hogarth, but they did not employ Blake on their grander engraving projects, such as the Shakespeare Gallery, then just beginning. Blake's talent for technical innovation in the graphic arts seemed to offer a solution to these commercial frustrations.

In about 1788, he developed a method of "Illuminated Printing," as he called it in a 1793 advertisement. According to Blake's earliest biographers, the technique was revealed in a dream by Blake's recently deceased and much-beloved younger brother, Robert. Visionary revelations may have played a role, but we can also see how the new approach to printmaking evolved out of the craft in which Blake had been trained. In conventional (or "intaglio") etching and engraving, the ink resides in and is printed from lines and dots incised into the copperplate. Blake's process, now generally called "relief etching," reverses this relationship and creates a metal plate with the printing characteristics of a woodcut. Blake began by drawing his pictures with a brush, or letters with a stylus, on a copperplate in an acid-resistant liquid that would harden quickly on contact with the metal. This liquid was very probably one of the "stop-out" varnishes used for intaglio etching. Letters had to be written backwards so that they would print right-way around, but this would have offered few problems for a skilled engraver. Blake next applied acid to the face of the plate, and this would eat away the unprotected metal to leave the images in shallow relief. White lines could be added to dark areas either by scratching through the varnish before etching or by cutting into the metal with an engraving tool after the application of acid. Having removed the stop-out material, Blake would ink the relief surfaces and print with light pressure in the engraver's rolling press he probably acquired during his partnership with Parker.

Blake must have found his new process appealing for several reasons, not the least of which were its simplicity and directness. Conventional printmaking in Blake's day, even when practiced by the artist who invented the designs, included the full development of the image on paper and its semimechanical transfer to the printing plate. In contrast, relief etching, like drawing or writing, was autographic, and allowed the artist/author to print multiple impressions of his own graphic gestures and handwriting created directly in the printing medium. In this respect, relief etching anticipates lithography, invented in Germany a few years later. The images produced by Blake's new technique had a rough and primitive quality that accorded with his aesthetic, which linked originality and origins, the new and the very old. By producing illustrated books in relief etching, assisted only by his wife, and selling directly to the public, Blake could avoid the commercial systems unreceptive to his efforts as an artist and writer. Blake kept his relief-etched plates throughout his life and returned to them several times to print new editions of his books.

Blake's earliest experiments in relief etching were probably motivated by a desire to produce facsimile drawings, but he very quickly began to integrate texts with his designs. His first illuminated book is *All Religions are One* of 1788, a series of emblems with accompanying aphorisms on ten small plates that sets forth some of his most basic thoughts on the sources of knowledge and art within what he called the "Poetic Genius." The unique copy of the work is in the Huntington Library (Illus. 1). *All Religions* was followed shortly by a companion series, *There is no Natural Religion,* that argues against rationalist deism. In the next year, Blake etched and printed his first book of illuminated poems, the *Songs of Innocence* (Illus. 2, 3). *The*

Book of Thel (Illus. 4, 5) also dates from 1789. We can find in this brief verse narrative the beginnings of Blake's mythological mode, indebted to Greek and Roman legends but extended into his own cast of characters and unique perspective on the origins and ends of human life. The Huntington copies of *Innocence* and *Thel* show the simple and delicate hand-tinting with watercolors that Blake used to illuminate his books during his early years of production. This coloring was done before the prints were assembled into separate volumes, and thus all copies from the same printing session tend to share the same palette and style, although the colors are often used in different arrangements (for example, a blue dress and a pink flower on one impression, the reverse in another). Catherine Blake participated in this work, but the extent and precise nature of her contribution have never been determined.

For Europeans, the 1790s were dominated by the French Revolution and its consequences. It seemed to many that, for good or ill, overwhelming forces of apocalyptic proportions had been released. Intellectuals in England and on the Continent began to question even the most basic assumptions about human nature and society, while others defended the old structures as the last bastion against chaos. Blake's work shows that he was caught up in this ferment in ways that energized his productivity—eight illuminated books in three years—but darkened his thoughts. In the late 1780s, Blake had become interested in the writings of the Swedish mystic Emanuel Swedenborg but soon found his ideas little more than conventional pieties or the repetition of concepts devised by earlier and greater thinkers. This rejection forms the core of Blake's most enthusiastic and varied illuminated book, *The Marriage of Heaven and Hell* (c. 1790), at once a humorous parody, a satanic extravagance, and a serious work of ideological analysis. The new intensity also makes itself felt in *Visions of the Daughters of Albion* of 1793 (Illus. 6, 7), an illuminated poem wrestling with the issues of sexuality, slavery, and liberation. The political landscape of the times, the titular subject of Blake's unillustrated *French Revolution*, again becomes an immediate issue in a series of three "Continent" books etched and first printed between 1793 and 1795: *America* (Illus. 8–10), *Europe*, and *The Song of Los*, the last divided into sections entitled "Africa" and "Asia" (Illus. 22–25). As was typical of Blake's thought, in these poems he placed contemporary struggles between the old order and the new energy within the broadest possible context, including biblical history, and viewed each event as part of universal cycles of time leading to apocalypse.

Blake's activities as a writer of illuminated books extended in two further directions during the mid–1790s. The *Songs of Experience* (1794) provide a contrary companion to the earlier *Songs of Innocence.* Blake first printed his new anthology of lyrics as a separate book but soon joined them under a general title page to create *Songs of Innocence and of Experience.* The Huntington's collection includes both the separate issue of *Experience* (Illus. 20, 21) and the combined *Songs* (Illus. 13–19). Several of the *Experience* poems treat the world as a prison for the human spirit, a perspective that Blake developed into the complex cosmic myth first presented in detail in *The Book of Urizen* (1794). Here we encounter the story of creation, fall, and struggle for restoration that would dominate Blake's poetry well into the next century. As the French Revolution descended into the Terror, Blake perceived that desire was thwarted not simply by the institutions of the state but by our most fundamental beliefs about time, space, and the self. What most of us still think of as unchangeable certainties about what constitutes reality, Blake saw as only one model of the universe—and a very unsatisfactory one at that. Salvation would come not from political revolution but a revolution in the mind, guided by neither nature nor reason but by the imagination, an attribute Blake would later identify with the labors of the artist and with the Christ within each man and woman.

The illuminated books of the 1790s show Blake's development as a printmaker as much as a poet. The relief etchings became larger and more sophisticated. The gentle, picturesque style of *Songs of Innocence* gave way to the sublime and terrific. Blake's art in this period was influenced by his friend Henry Fuseli, a Swiss-German artist working in London whose extravagant and often erotic images were matched by a wide knowledge of literature and Renaissance art. Both men were indebted to Michelangelo for their expressive treatment of the human body. We also find a concomitant shift in Blake's habits as a colorist. In 1794 he began to paint the designs on his relief-etched plates with opaque pigments and to print these along with the accompanying inked texts. Even *All Religions are One* (Illus. 1) shows small amounts of this color printing from relief surfaces, but Blake soon found that he could print from etched shallows or even from unetched plates. This technique, always subject to accident and variation, produced reticulated patches of color that required work with brush and pen on each impression to restore essential outlines. The Huntington's *Song of Los* (Illus. 22–25) is one of the finest examples of this rich, impasto coloring style. During this same period, Blake's hand-coloring developed in a similar direction toward darker and denser effects. The finished designs look more like paintings than tinted prints.

Modern interest in the illuminated books tends to overemphasize their importance within Blake's career. Even during his most intensive production of illuminated books, from 1789 to 1795, Blake did not abandon more conventional media. He continued to execute watercolors and a few intaglio prints based on his own designs. The Huntington possesses two of these exceedingly rare prints, *Albion rose* and *Lucifer and the Pope in Hell* (Illus. 11, 12). Both are strikingly color printed from the surfaces of the copperplates rather than the incised lines. This technique rapidly evolved into Blake's twelve large color prints, first produced in 1795 and thought by some to be his supreme achievement in the visual arts. Many of these, including the example of *Hecate* at the Huntington (Illus. 26), were probably printed from millboard rather than metal plates.

At about the same time that Blake developed his relief etching and color printing to their fullest expression, he began two ambitious projects—one commercial, the other decidedly not. The bookseller Richard Edwards hired Blake to illustrate a sumptuous edition of Edward Young's *Night Thoughts*, a long, lugubrious, but then very popular poem. With what must have been extraordinary energy and discipline, in about two years Blake produced 537 watercolors to surround the letterpress text of Young's poem. Unfortunately, only the first four of nine "Nights" (as Young titled the sections of his poem) were published. Like several other graphic projects, Edwards's edition had fallen prey to a depressed market for prints, due in part to the embargo on exports to the Continent because of the growing conflict between England and France.

While Blake the artist was illustrating Young's poem, Blake the poet began an epic narrative of his own nocturnal visions, also divided into "Nights." This work, which he first titled *Vala* and later changed to *The Four Zoas,* was Blake's attempt to create one vast, totalizing myth to sum up his understanding of human consciousness—its origins, internal conflicts, fragmentation, and projections into the world of time and space. He continued to work on the illustrated manuscript for the next decade but never found a means for its publication.

By the end of the century, Blake's prospects were not bright. The failure of the *Night Thoughts* project, the generally depressed state of commercial engraving, and the incomplete state of *The Four Zoas* must have taken their toll. With enthusiasm and high hopes, Blake in 1800 accepted an invitation from the well-known writer William Hayley to move to Felpham near the English Channel to work on a variety of art projects, including the decoration of Hayley's library with panel paintings and the engraving of illustrations for his forthcoming books. Blake was initially pleased with his new patron, but the relationship gradually descended into frustration and recrimination on both sides. The final blow was provided by a drunken soldier, John Scolfield, whom Blake physically ejected from his garden. In revenge, Scolfield formally charged Blake with sedition for having damned the king (as Blake may very well have done while contending with one of the king's soldiers). Blake, who had returned to London in the fall of 1803, was found innocent in January 1804. But the affair shook his conceptions of self and community. Even though Hayley had generously supported Blake during the trial, Blake seems to have associated his patron with the forces of conspiratorial repression. For the next dozen or so years, Blake became a more isolated figure, while his poetry and designs moved even further from the mainstream of contemporary tastes. It is all too easy to romanticize cultural alienation into a necessary condition for genius to flourish, but Blake's meager income and lack of a receptive audience probably did more harm than good to his art.

As Blake's letters reveal, he descended into periods of depression during and shortly after his residence near Hayley. Yet the Felpham years were not without productive consequences. Blake's spiritual crises provided materials for *The Four Zoas,* but that work proved incapable of containing his visions of struggle and renewal. He returned instead to illuminated printing and began, no later than 1804, to write and etch two epic poems, *Milton* and *Jerusalem.* The first weaves into mythic form the complex relationships among various aspects of Blake's own character, Hayley (figured in the text as Satan), and the great Christian poet, John Milton, whose work inspired Blake's own but whose supposed errors needed correction. The Huntington is fortunate in having a beautifully colored copy of *Milton* (Illus. 37–41), one of only four Blake is known to have produced.

Drawing and painting remained central to Blake's life throughout the Felpham interlude. Shortly before leaving London, he began to execute for his patron, Thomas Butts, a series of paintings illustrating the Bible. By 1803, Blake had completed over fifty of these works, executed in a medium generally called "tempera" but probably a glue- or gum-based paint similar to his color-printing material. Between 1800 and 1805, Blake also produced for Butts a group of about eighty-five watercolors also illustrating events in the Old and New Testaments. The Huntington's collection includes one example from each series, the tempera of *Lot and His Daughters* (Illus. 27) and the dramatic watercolor *The Conversion of Saul* (Illus. 28).

As work on the Bible illustrations proceeded, Blake began to execute on commission—first for a new patron, Joseph Thomas, and then for Butts—several series of illustrations to some of Milton's most famous poems. The designs for *Comus, Paradise Lost,* and "On the Morning of Christ's Nativity," all acquired by Henry Huntington in 1914 and 1916, now form the heart of the Art Gallery's collection of Blake's watercolors. The three series, plus the magnificent *Satan, Sin, and Death* from a second group of *Paradise Lost* designs, are reproduced complete in this volume (Illus. 29–36, 42–54, 56–61). Along with the illuminated book *Milton,* these designs offer intriguing insights into Blake's responses to the man he saw as a poetic father, brother, and at times even adversary.

The visual components of Blake's illuminated books often stray, in remarkably fruitful ways, from the words they accompany, or offer a parallel but alternative "text" in pictorial form. In contrast, the Milton designs, like most of Blake's illustrations to the works of other writers, remain exceptionally close to the text. Yet this fidelity can produce startling effects because of Blake's habit of translating verbal metaphors into pictures. The usual distinctions between the literal and the figural, between visual reality and imagination, are thereby disconcerted. The result is an illustrative style we might term "visionary literalism." At the same time, it is possible to coordinate motifs in the Milton or Bible illustrations with equivalents, pictorial or literary, in the illuminated books and to interpret Blake's designs as critical commentaries on the texts illustrated.

Blake's return to London in 1803 renewed his spirits but not his commercial prospects. As he wrote to Hayley after a month back in the great city, "Art in London flourishes. Engravers in particular are wanted. . . . Yet no one brings work to me." Thus, Blake must have been delighted when the engraver and would-be book publisher Robert Cromek came to him in September 1805 with a commission to prepare illustrations for a handsome edition of Robert Blair's poem *The Grave.* Blake quickly drew a number of striking designs, including several never published (Illus. 55), but Cromek found Blake's sample etching to be too crude and transferred the lucrative commission to engrave the designs to the fashionable craftsman Louis Schiavonetti. Blake's sense of betrayal grew into a belief that Cromek had stolen from him the idea to paint and engrave a picture of Geoffrey Chaucer's "Canterbury Pilgrims" setting out on their journey and had given that task to Blake's old friend Stothard. Blake felt that friends both old and new were arrayed against him.

Public failures and private distresses dogged Blake and his wife for the next decade. His exhibition of paintings in 1809, held at his older brother's house, is not known to have resulted in any sales and attracted only a single, damning review in which Robert Hunt accused Blake of being "an unfortunate lunatic." Even Blake's friends seem to have been bewildered by the *Descriptive Catalogue* Blake prepared for his show; but this rare booklet, a copy of which is in the Huntington Library, is now appreciated as one of Blake's most important statements on his theories of art and its history. Three years later, Blake joined the Associated Painters in Water-Colours and placed three paintings, including his Canterbury Pilgrims panorama, in their 1812 exhibition. Even this attempt at reaching a wider audience resulted in a fiasco: the Associated Painters could not pay the rent for the exhibition hall, and the landlord seized many of the works on display. During the next half-dozen years, Blake managed to obtain a few commercial engraving commissions, mostly through the kind efforts of Flaxman, to paint and draw more designs for Butts, and to work on the one hundred plates of *Jerusalem*, not completed until 1820. But none of these efforts could attract public recognition beyond a small coterie. Blake had become an obscure figure, even for those conversant with London's art world.

Blake's fortunes began to change in 1818. An up-and-coming artist, John Linnell, heard about Blake, visited him, and hired him to help engrave a portrait. From this humble beginning, Linnell's friendship and patronage grew into a crucial influence in the final, and very productive, decade of Blake's life. Of equal importance was Linnell's role in introducing Blake to a group of young artists, including Samuel Palmer, Edward Calvert, and George Richmond, all of whose works are well represented at the Huntington. They fell under Blake's spell and took an almost worshipful attitude toward the man they called "The Interpreter." Artistic brotherhood, a theme in Blake's writings but an ideal unachieved through most of his life, found a happy conclusion in a version of artistic fatherhood. Blake, as a patriarchal figure in his sixties, acquired an audience of fellow artists who gave him renewed confidence and sense of purpose.

Linnell also introduced Blake to John Varley, a landscape painter whose interests extended into the pseudosciences of physiognomy and astrology. At Varley's behest, Blake would call before his mind's eye the faces of men and women from the past and sketch their portraits. The Huntington has nine of these drawings, including one of the few picturing the body as well as the visage (Illus. 62). More than any of his other designs, these "Visionary Heads" raise complex issues surrounding Blake's claims that he could directly apprehend a reality beyond the senses. According to Alexander Gilchrist (see "For Further Reading," below), when still a child Blake saw a tree filled with angels. Similar experiences came to Blake throughout his life and were intertwined with acts of projective imagination he believed to be intrinsic to all artistic creation. Such habits of mind, as well as Blake's tendency to confound the customary distinctions between material and imaginary experiences, and between metaphoric and literal modes of discourse, resemble certain forms of schizophrenia. But whether or not Blake's brain had an unusual chemistry, his importance rests upon what he did with his visions. Many people diverge from the psychic norms of their society; few create great poems and pictures.

With the completion of *Jerusalem*, Blake brought his illuminated poetry to a spectacular conclusion. It was not, however, the last of his etched and engraved texts. Between 1822 and 1826, he produced three brief works that sum up his final views on atonement and forgiveness, the relations between art and commerce, and the unity of imagination and religious faith. *The Ghost of Abel* on two plates and *On Homers Poetry* [and] *On Virgil* on a single plate were etched in relief; one of just three complete copies of the former is in the Huntington's collection. In the final work, Blake surrounded with bold aphorisms a carefully drawn reproduction of the classical statue the *Laocoön*, and he executed this unusual compound as a single intaglio plate. This engraving participates in a return to traditional graphic techniques that characterizes Blake's most important endeavors in his final years. He revised many of his earlier engravings, including *Albion rose* (see Illus. 11 for the earlier version) and a book of captioned emblems entitled *For Children: The Gates of Paradise* that had been first printed in 1793. In late copies of *For Children*, such as the one at the Huntington, the work has been transformed both visually and verbally into *For the Sexes: The Gates of Paradise.*

Commissions from Linnell and his friends led to the creation of Blake's final masterpieces in the graphic arts, the Virgil, Job, and Dante engravings. All three are represented by fine impressions in the Huntington collection. For R. J. Thornton's school text of Virgil's pastorals, Blake first etched four illustrations in relief on metal. The boldly primitive designs and their unconventional medium were unacceptable to Thornton and his publishers. But this was the most fortunate rejection in Blake's career, for it led to his creation of seventeen small wood engravings published in the third (1821) edition of the textbook. These small blocks had a profound influence on Palmer and Calvert and are now considered by many to be among the greatest wood engravings produced by a British artist. Two years later, Blake began to engrave the illustrations to the Book of Job he had first produced as a series of watercolors in about 1805. The twenty-two plates present, in pictures and surrounding quotations from many books of the Bible, the life of Job as a universal tale of error, suffering, forgiveness, and redemption. The peace that comes at the end of Job's life may be Blake's reflection on his own, or at least on what he hoped it to be. The Job illustrations are Blake's greatest work as an engraver.

Blake began, in about 1824, to suffer fevers and shivering fits caused by the gallstones that would eventually kill him. Nonetheless, he carried on with his art. Even before finishing the Job series late in 1825, Blake had begun the much larger project of illustrating Dante's *Divine Comedy.* He prepared a series of 102 drawings and watercolors and from these selected seven designs for engraving. Blake did not live to finish even one of these large plates, but what we have gives some indication of the continued strength of his eye and hand. Several other projects remained incomplete at Blake's death, including designs based on John Bunyan's *Pilgrim's Progress,* a large watercolor titled *Moses Placed in the Ark of the Bulrushes* (Illus. 63), and a manuscript of the Book of Genesis. In the last, now in the Huntington's collection, Blake reached back to a form even older than engraving—the illuminated manuscript (Illus. 64). Thus, near the end of his days, Blake was transcribing and illustrating the beginning of the Bible, the book that had shaped his life and art more than any other.

Blake died on August 12, 1827. George Richmond was at his bedside and reported in a letter to Palmer that, in his last minutes, Blake "burst out into Singing of the things he saw in Heaven." In a skeptical age like ours, such reports are often taken to be maudlin, if not fictive. Yet we have reason for believing Richmond and sensing the justice of such an ending for Blake, in light of the character of the works he has left us. Some of the best portions of that legacy, preserved by Henry Huntington and the institution he founded, appear on the pages that follow.

A NOTE ON BLAKE'S ILLUMINATED BOOKS

Every known copy of each of Blake's illuminated books has been assigned a letter (copy A, copy B, etc.) by modern scholars. These designations are recorded in G. E. Bentley, Jr., *Blake Books* (1977), and are given here in the headings for the illuminated books reproduced. Blake issued many of his illuminated books, particularly the lyric anthologies *Songs of Innocence* and *Songs of Experience*, with different arrangements of the plates. The standard plate numbers recorded in Bentley's *Blake Books* are followed here.

Plates and Commentaries

1

All Religions are One, frontispiece, copy A. Relief etching, central image 2 x 1½″ (5.2 x 3.6 cm). Etched 1788, color printed and with pen drawing added on the impression c. 1795. Call no. 57445

Blake's first illuminated book begins with a young man, nude except for a cloth over his left leg, seated in a forest and pointing with both arms to the right. Inscribed below is "The Voice of one crying in the Wilderness." This caption (quoted from all four Gospels of the Bible), the setting, and the youth's gestures identify him as John the Baptist. Much as the biblical figure directed his audience to the coming of Christ, his portrayal here directs us into Blake's book. There we find a sequence of nine similarly small plates, adorned with designs and brief aphorisms setting forth, in almost syllogistic form, Blake's argument that all religions are indeed one because all are expressions of the "Poetic Genius," the universal imagination that is also the god within each person. The human body and human institutions, such as religions, are outward manifestations of this inner power. Given such a context for the man pictured here, he can also be identified with Blake himself, the author of this book who, in a forest of unbelief, leads us to what he believes to be a spiritual revelation.

Blake no doubt pulled at least some proofs of *All Religions are One* shortly after he etched it, but no such impressions exist today. The Huntington's copy, the only one extant, includes all but the title plate and was printed by Blake some seven years after etching as part of a large-format edition of several of his illuminated books. The pen-and-ink framing lines may have been added even later. The volume remained in the collection of Blake's great patron John Linnell and his heirs until its sale at auction to Henry Huntington in 1918.

2.

Songs of Innocence, "The Shepherd," copy I. Relief etching with white-line etching/engraving, 4⅛ x 2¾" (11.1 x 6.9 cm). Etched, printed, and hand-colored 1789. Call no. 54040

Blake's first book of illuminated poetry offers brief lyrics and accompanying designs that evoke a childhood world prior to the dualisms of adult consciousness. From this perspective, there are no divisions between child and nature, the human and the divine. But language is itself based on lexical distinctions and thus threatens the state of innocence in the very act of representing it. The artful simplicity of Blake's words, rhythms, and pictures attempts to preserve these vulnerable glimpses of Eden from the encroachments of experience.

"The Shepherd" stresses a balanced relationship between man and beast, one in which the shepherd is a gentle guardian but is himself led by the sheep "all the day." He is the fatherly equivalent of the ewes who reply tenderly to the lambs' "innocent call." Elsewhere in *Songs of Innocence*, both the lamb and the shepherd take on their traditional biblical meanings as metaphors for Christ as the incarnate god within nature. The design also evokes sympathetic communication, for one sheep (perhaps a lamb) looks toward the shepherd, who returns the gaze. His elegant contrapposto posture, based on Classical and Renaissance precedents, is echoed by the flowering vine entwined about the tree on the right, a traditional emblem for marriage. Such mutually supportive and fruitful unions are also suggested by the flock of sheep, pictured almost as a single creature with many backs. A large bird soars upward on the left as a pictorial equivalent for the shepherd's "praise"—and for Blake's song.

Copy I of the *Songs of Innocence* is from the first printing. Its delicate, understated hand-tinting is in keeping with the tone of the poems and is typical of Blake's style for all his illuminated books until about 1794. Blake sang his *Songs* to tunes of his own composition, but his music was never transcribed.

See Illus. 14 and 15 for the frontispiece and title page to *Songs of Innocence*.

3.

Songs of Innocence, "Infant Joy," copy I. Relief etching, 4⅜ x 2¾″ (11.1 x 6.8 cm).
Etched, printed, and hand-colored 1789.

Although one of Blake's simplest evocations of innocence, "Infant Joy" touches on the complex issue of naming as an act that leads from childhood to the adult world. Perhaps innocence is preserved by the fact that the adult, whom we hear in lines 3, 6, and 7–12, does not impose a name but only confirms the self-christening and blessing magically pronounced by the infant (etymologically, one "without speech") in the first stanza:

> *I happy am*
> *Joy is my name,—*
> *Sweet joy befall thee!*

The graceful curves of the design recall medieval Celtic decorations and anticipate the Art Nouveau style of the late nineteenth century. The scene unfolding within the womblike flower, probably influenced by Renaissance portrayals of the Adoration of Christ, unites botanical, animal, human, and divine states of being. The standing figure is positioned like the flower's pistil, while her dotted wings suggest those of both a fertilizing insect and the classical goddess Psyche, representative of the soul (see also Illus. 55). These pictorial metaphors complement the unions of feeling ("happy") and name ("Joy"), of infant expression and adult response, playing through the poem's interwoven voices. Is the pendant flower on the right latent with another nativity, or is it an image of decay?

The plate is the most richly colored in this copy of *Innocence.* In copy E of the combined *Songs,* also at the Huntington, both flowers are a somber blue.

A young shepherdess, burdened by her sense of mortality, sets out to find a meaning for her life by talking with several creatures—a lily, cloud, worm, and clod of clay. These speaking symbols of life's transience are satisfied with their lot because all believe themselves to be part of natural cycles related through self-sacrifice to a spiritual purpose. On the final plate, the poem's gentle pastoralism shifts abruptly to the horrific sublime as Thel comes to her own grave and hears unanswered questions redolent with fears of both death and sexuality. This voice, and Thel's flight from it, indicate either her failure to accept the harsh truths of life or the failure of the characters she meets to satisfy the human desire for transcendental truths.

Thel's character, the tone of her poem, and its central themes are indicated by the title-page design, unrelated to any specific passage in the text. The men and women inhabiting the title letters, the soaring birds and human figures, and even the vegetation seem caught up in joyful activities in which Thel never participates. She stands meekly on the left, an observer of a scene that, for all its pictorial delicacy, suggests sexual strife. A male grasps a female about the waist. Are her arms raised in joy or fear? Is this lovers' play or a rape? Such questions haunt Thel throughout her poem. If interpreted as the human forms of the flowers below them, the couple may be a personification of pollination—a rather extravagant conceit, but precisely the sort developed in Erasmus Darwin's *The Loves of the Plants*, a poem published in the same year as the date (1789) on Blake's title page and very probably known to him. Equally worrisome are the questions raised by the arching tree. Is it protective, or does it outline the shape of a tombstone bearing Thel's name?

Thel's posture recalls the Medici Venus, but the design's general stylistic qualities have more in common with the work of Blake's friend Thomas Stothard whose *Zephyrus and Flora*, engraved by Blake in 1784, pictures a scene similar to the one Thel witnesses.

5.

The Book of Thel, plate 7, copy L. Relief etching, 6¹/₈ x 4¹/₄″ (15.4 x 10.6 cm). Etched 1789, printed and hand-colored late 1789 or early 1790.

Thel, seated and with arms folded protectively over her breasts, gazes down upon the human forms of the "matron Clay" and the infant Worm (see commentary on Illus. 4 for these characters). This design on the penultimate plate of the book juxtaposes Thel's clothed body and enclosed posture with the languorous nudity of the Clay (reminiscent of a Renaissance Venus) and the energetic gestures of the Worm. The exotic vegetation seems rank or even menacing, like the giant, sexualized plants in the paintings of Hieronymus Bosch. The Worm and Clay are described on plate 6 in a way similar to their presentation here, but there are no direct points of textual contact for the other motifs in the design.

The stylized coloring of the sky in the Huntington copy, and particularly the mustard-colored clouds, add a further note of unnaturalness to the pastoral scene below. Blake painted water just above the lower margin and on the left in three copies, thereby suggesting that the three characters are on an island.

But he that loves the lowly, pours his oil upon my head,
And kisses me, and binds his nuptial bands around my breast.
And says; Thou mother of my children, I have loved thee.
And I have given thee a crown that none can take away:
But how this is sweet maid, I know not, and I cannot know,
I ponder, and I cannot ponder; yet I live and love.

The daughter of beauty wip'd her pitying tears with her white veil,
And said. Alas! I knew not this, and therefore did I weep:
That God would love a Worm I knew, and punish the evil foot
That wilful, bruis'd its helpless form: but that he cherish'd it
With milk and oil, I never knew; and therefore did I weep,
And I complaind in the mild air, because I fade away.
And lay me down in thy cold bed, and leave my shining lot.

Queen of the vales, the matron Clay answerd; I heard thy sighs,
And all thy moans flew oer my roof, but I have calld them down:
Wilt thou O Queen enter my house, tis given thee to enter.
And to return; fear nothing, enter with thy virgin feet.

5

IV

6.

Oothoon, the heroine of *Visions*, plucks the "flower" of sexual fulfillment at the beginning of the poem but is soon raped by a brutal slavemaster, Bromion. Her lover, Theotormon, responds with silence or useless abstractions. But this slender plot is only a thread on which Blake hangs Oothoon's questionings of conventional wisdom and practices. She insists on her inner purity and, in a long concluding lament to the "Daughters of Albion" (that is, the women of England), on the varieties of energetic self-expression that cannot be delimited by legalistic repression. These themes may have been influenced by the life and writings of Mary Wollstonecraft, one of whose books Blake illustrated in 1791. But Oothoon, in contrast to the author of *A Vindication of the Rights of Woman* (1792), stresses passion, not reason. The poem's stormy rhetoric and the characters' names continue the tradition of James Macpherson's Celtic fabrications, the works of Ossian, thought by Blake and many others of his time to be genuine translations from ancient songs.

The frontispiece is a visual exploration of a passage on plate 5:

> *Then storms rent Theotormons limbs; he rolld his waves around.*
> *And folded his black jealous waters round the adulterate pair*
> *Bound back to back in Bromions caves terror & meekness dwell*
> *At entrance Theotormon sits wearing the threshold hard*

The back-to-back manacling of Oothoon and her tormentor picture the text's harsh criticism of marriage, the woman "bound / In spells of law to one she loaths." Bromion is terrified by some unseen presence to the left, while Theotormon (a pun on "tormented of god"?) is totally self-enclosed. The cave's mouth has its own horrific physiognomy, like that of a skull seen in profile and looking to the left, its eye socket formed by the sun peeking through clouds. This perspective transforms the characters into the human forms of imprisoned mental states.

The simple coloring of the first-edition impressions, like the one at the Huntington, is perhaps less effective in emphasizing the dark power of the etched image than the dense color printing Blake used for several examples he produced a year or two later.

7.

Visions of the Daughters of Albion, title page, copy E. Relief etching with touches of white-line etching/ engraving, 6⅜ x 5⅛″ (16.3 x 12.9 cm). Etched, printed, and hand-colored 1793.

In this complex and storm-tossed design, Blake pictures many of the forces contending in the text. Oothoon flees over dark waves and looks back at a winged and fiery monster in hot pursuit. His action indicates he is the rapist Bromion, but his arms wrapped about his shoulders suggest the self-enclosure of Theotormon (see commentary on Illus. 6 for these characters). Perhaps he is a composite of both males and thus a pictorial prototype of Urizen (see Illus. 9), the evil demiurge in Blake's mythological poetry named for the first time in *Visions.* To the left, a ring of female dancers (personified joys?) seems about to be broken by the pursuer's wing. The figures on the clouds above are far less energetic, as though already encumbered by woe or worse. The man in the upper right gestures as if he were the source of the rain cascading over the cliffs below. These look like old men in some copies, their heads between hunched shoulders. A few etched lines indicate a rainbow arching through the center of the title. In most impressions, including the Huntington's, the printed outline has been emphasized with a rainbow of colors. Is this a hopeful image, or merely a parody of the sign of God's covenant in Genesis? The motto beneath Oothoon—"The Eye sees more than the Heart knows"—points to a gap between perception and knowledge, one of many destructive or delimiting disjunctions in the poem.

8.

America a Prophecy, frontispiece, copy I. Relief and white-line etching, probably with some white-line engraving, 9¼ x 6⅝″ (23.4 x 16.9 cm). Etched and printed 1793. Call no. 54044

America is the first of Blake's "Continent" books (see also *The Song of Los,* Illus. 22–25) in which he explores the recent American and French revolutions, places them in the context of biblical prophecy and Ossianic imagery, and projects an impending apocalypse that will reconfigure nature itself.

The frontispiece does not illustrate a specific passage but epitomizes the whole with an image of war's consequences. The haft of a broken sword and a dismounted cannon lie in the foreground. Perhaps the latter blasted the hole in the stony, and classically embellished, wall behind. Escape through the breach is blocked by a shackled angel with enormous wings. He may be "Albions Angel" in the poem, a representative of the establishment forces of counter-revolution. Alternatively, he may be Orc, the spirit of revolt who is described as chained and with face hidden at the beginning of the poem. These and other points of intersection with the text suggest that the figure is not a single named character but the representation of a physical and mental condition, the "inchained soul," to which both contending ideologies have led. A woman and two children, like refugees from the *Songs of Innocence,* huddle together before the ruins of empire. Storm clouds swag in the sky.

Blake seems originally to have intended *America,* with its detailed white-line work that hand-coloring would conceal, as a book to be issued only in monochrome copies. None of the ten copies produced in the first printing of 1793 was initially colored by Blake (one copy was colored at a later time, perhaps by Catherine Blake).

9.

America a Prophecy, plate 10, copy I. Relief etching with white-line etching/engraving,
9¼ x 6⅝" (23.5 x 16.7 cm). Etched and printed 1793.

Orc, the spirit of revolution, announces the renewal of "fiery joy" in the text, but his words are written on a cloud suspended between dark waters of the Atlantic and the domineering figure of Urizen, the
creator of the fallen world and a Moses-like promulgator of its laws. He is a skygod "who sat / Above all
heavens in thunders wrap'd" (plate 18). His name puns on both "your reason" and the Greek word for
"horizon," respectively for Blake the primary mental and physical limitations encumbering human vision.
Urizen's cloudy realm is at once both material and insubstantial, like the abstractions of rationalist science
and natural religion Blake abhorred. See Illus. 10 for the contrasting portrayal of Orc, and Illus. 38 for a
more vulnerable Urizen.

The terror answerd: I am Orc. wreath'd round the accursed tree:
The times are ended; shadows pass the morning gins to break:
The fiery joy, that Urizen perverted to ten commands,
What night he led the starry hosts thro' the wide wilderness:
That stony law I stamp to dust: and scatter religion abroad
To the four winds as a torn book, & none shall gather the leaves;
But they shall rot on desart sands, & consume in bottomless deeps,
To make the desarts blossom, & the deeps shrink to their fountains,
And to renew the fiery joy, and burst the stony roof.
That pale religious letchery, seeking Virginity,
May find it in a harlot, and in coarse-clad honesty
The undefil'd tho' ravish'd in her cradle night and morn:
For every thing that lives is holy, life delights in life;
Because the soul of sweet delight can never be defil'd.
Fires inwrap the earthly globe, yet man is not consumd;
Amidst the lustful fires he walks; his feet become like brass,
His knees and thighs like silver, & his breast and head like gold.

10

America a Prophecy, plate 12, copy I. Relief and white-line etching perhaps with touches of white-line engraving, 9¼ x 5⅝" (23.5 x 16.9 cm). Etched and printed 1793.

Orc, the passionate revolutionary, rises from the underworld in flames that seem about to devour the text above. His devilish powers are emphasized by snaky locks. The moment is described on plate 14: "the Demon red, who burnt towards America, / . . . Breaking in smoky wreaths from the wild deep, & gath'ring thick / In flames as of a furnace on the land from North to South." Coming only two plates after Urizen's portrayal on plate 10 (Illus. 9), the design forges a dramatic contrast between fire and water, rising and descending energies, youth and age. Orc's posture, a mirror image of Urizen's, continues the oppositional structure; but it may also suggest that the two figures are bound together, like positive and negative electric charges that cannot exist without their opposite. As companion designs, plates 10 and 12 visualize the Blakean dialectic most directly presented in *The Marriage of Heaven and Hell:* "Without Contraries is no progression. Attraction and Repulsion, Reason and Energy, Love and Hate, are necessary to Human existence" (plate 3).

Thus wept the Angel voice & as he wept the terrible blasts
Of trumpets, blew a loud alarm across the Atlantic deep.
No trumpets answer; no reply of clarions or of fifes,
Silent the Colonies remain and refuse the loud alarm.

On those vast shady hills between America & Albions shore;
Now barr'd out by the Atlantic sea: call'd Atlantean hills:
Because from their bright summits you may pass to the Golden world
An ancient palace, archetype of mighty Emperies,
Rears its immortal pinnacles, built in the forest of God
By Ariston the king of beauty for his stolen bride.

Here on their magic seats the thirteen Angels sat perturb'd
For clouds from the Atlantic hover o'er the solemn roof.

Albion rose (or *Glad Day* or *The Dance of Albion*). Intaglio etching/engraving, first state, 10³/₄ x 7 ⅞″
(27.2 x 19.9 cm). Etched c. 1793, color printed from the surface of the plate and hand-colored c. 1796.
Accession no. 000.124

The iconography of Blake's image of liberated human potential changed significantly through its long compositional history. His c. 1780 pencil sketches of the youth from front and rear were probably based on an engraving of a Roman statuette or Vetruvian figures showing ideal human proportions. Although an academic exercise at this point, the design may also be a spiritual self-portrait associated with the end of Blake's apprenticeship and the beginning of his career as an engraver. The first state of the etching/engraving, known only from intaglio lines we can see beneath the color printing of the Huntington's impression, can be dated to c. 1793 on stylistic grounds. In that context, the design can be associated with Orc, the embodiment of revolutionary energy (see Illus. 10). As part of his so-called *Large Book of Designs,* a 1796 selection of prints without accompanying texts, Blake color printed the plate planographically. The first of these impressions is in the British Museum; the second, with thinner colors, is the one reproduced here. The sunburst behind, or emanating from, the figure associates him with Los, the representative of the active imagination in Blake's mythological poetry (see Illus. 25).

Blake returned to the engraving sometime after 1803—perhaps as late as the 1820s, when he reworked many of his earlier intaglio graphics. He added lines of radiance and burnishing around the figure and, beneath his feet, a worm and bat-winged moth as creatures of darkness dispelled by the human sun. Although it may appear beneath the surface colors of the first state, only impressions of the second state reveal the inscription "WB inv 1780" (meaning that Blake first "invented" the image in that year). A new caption appears beneath the design: "Albion rose from where he labourd at the Mill with Slaves / Giving himself for the Nations he danc'd the dance of Eternal Death." In his final incarnation, the youth striding above the earth is identified as Albion, a traditional name for Britain but in Blake's later poetry the personification of all humanity. He arises from the trammels of fallen time and space in a heroic act of self-sacrifice.

12.

Lucifer and the Pope in Hell. Intaglio etching/engraving, 7 ¼ x 9 ¾" (18.3 x 24.6 cm). Etched c. 1794, color printed from the surface of the plate and hand-colored c. 1795–96. Accession no. 000.125

A group of crowned monarchs and their soldiers sink into hellish ground with flames behind. A serpent's coils wrap about one sufferer. A gowned pope, wearing his triple tiara, is led into bondage by a scaly devil. But this latest victim of satanic energy is not the Catholic pope, for his bald head and heavy brow, lips, jowls, and nose indicate that he is a caricature of the Anglican equivalent, King George III (compare James Gillray's *The Hopes of the Party,* in which George is being led to execution by three of his political adversaries). The design continues Blake's political themes of the early 1790s in which he predicts the overthrow of established institutions at the hands of forces conservatives consider devilish.

In an impression in the British Museum, printed in intaglio, the devil holds a chain attached to the pope's arm. More victims and serpent coils appear to their right. These motifs are covered by thick pigments in the Huntington impression, the only known colored example. The conjectural dating of the intaglio plate is based on its graphic style and political themes.

During or shortly after his production of *Songs of Experience* in 1794, Blake decided to unite the new work with the *Songs of Innocence*, etched five years earlier. The combined *Songs* encompass two visions of life, each reflecting on the other through comparisons and contrasts among their verbal and visual motifs. The subtitle on the general title page—"Shewing the Two Contrary States of the Human Soul"—indicates that Blake's images of child and adult are meant to be metaphors for a more fundamental distinction within the human psyche. Reading and viewing the work become explorations of our own minds as we shift between its two perspectives.

The design on the general title page pictures the expulsion of Adam and Eve, that moment in biblical history when the first man and woman have just been cast from the garden of innocence into the world of experience. The flames of divine wrath thrust Adam and Eve outward and downward, their bodies poised between the unclothed freedom of innocence (Illus. 14) and the enclosed postures of experience (Illus. 6, 18). Similarly, the vines about their loins are midway between innocent nudity and the heavy clothing Blake uses to indicate repression (Illus. 21). Eve's face, turned toward us in the etched image, is in this and several other impressions obscured by her hair. Like Adam, she looks down to the earth, their future grave. Yet we can find at least one motif to raise our spirits. The bird of song in the upper right may be a phoenix, the legendary creature born of fire whose presence can shift our interpretation of the flames from the wrathful to the restorative.

The Huntington's copy of the combined *Songs* has a complex production history. Most plates were printed in shades of raw sienna or yellow-ocher, but nine are in green. In spite of this variety, nearly all plates come from the first printings (1789, 1794) of each section and were hand-colored shortly thereafter. But the copy was not assembled until considerably later, probably in 1806 for Blake's major patron, Thomas Butts. At that time, Blake added further coloring to give a sense of visual unity to the copy. Several of the texts were poorly printed, and these Blake repaired with pen and ink.

14.

Songs of Innocence and of Experience, frontispiece to *Innocence,* copy E. Relief etching, with slight touches of white-line etching/engraving, 4³/₈ x 2³/₄″ (11 x 7 cm). Etched, printed, and hand-colored 1789, probably retouched c. 1806.

The frontispiece to *Innocence* illustrates the "Introduction" poem. The moment pictured corresponds to the third stanza when the child "on a cloud" commands the shepherd-piper, a spokesman for innocence throughout the anthology, to "drop [his] pipe" and "sing [his] songs of happy chear." He strides toward us, but looks back and up to a celestial child of heroic physique. The piper is a persona for Blake himself, inspired by a vision of idealized innocence to write these songs that "every child"—of any age—"may joy to hear." Unlike his muse, the piper is clothed, but we can still see the lineaments of "the human form divine" (see the text in Illus. 16) beneath his diaphanous body stocking. The flock of sheep, perhaps a semblance of an innocent audience, grazes contentedly within a tree-protected bower. Most early impressions are colored with hues in accord with the tone of the etched image and the poem it illustrates. The tinting in this example is unusually dark, as though the shadows of experience are already beginning to extend over the pastoral green.

The general disposition of the two figures and their iconography were probably influenced by the frontispiece to J. C. Lavater's *Aphorisms on Man,* designed by Blake's friend Henry Fuseli and engraved by Blake in 1788. See Illus. 17 for the contrasting frontispiece to *Experience.*

15

Songs of Innocence and of Experience, title page to *Innocence,* copy E. Relief etching and white-line etching/engraving, 4¼ x 3″ (12 x 7.4 cm). Etched, printed, and hand-colored 1789, probably retouched c. 1806.

An adult reading to or lecturing children is a common motif in frontispieces and title-page vignettes of eighteenth-century children's books. Blake exploits this convention by making one significant revision: the heavily dressed mother or nurse *shows* the book (a copy of these illustrated *Songs?*) to the boy and girl. The gnarled apple tree bears large fruit, colored an unripe green in this impression but golden or red in others. The vine twisting about the trunk is a traditional emblem of marriage (see also Illus. 2); but if we perceive the composition with the eyes of experience, we can see foreshadowed here the satanic serpent wrapped about the Tree of the Knowledge of Good and Evil in the Garden of Eden. Innocence and experience are comprised of what the reader brings to Blake's songs as well as what the poet gives to us.

Blake's persona, the shepherd-piper introduced on the frontispiece (Illus. 14), leans against the first letter of "Innocence." Other figures and birds sport about the title; a winged angel leans against the "n" of "Songs" and holds a book or tablet. The letters of "Songs" grow into flamelike leaves, colored red or orange in a few copies, to suggest a seamless union of word and world. Perhaps we are to think that the woman's elegant chair is made of wicker, and thus in keeping with this outdoor scene. As with the frontispiece in this copy of the combined *Songs,* the general coloring effect is atypically somber. Is the rosy hue in the sky an indication of dawn or dusk? Once again, how we see determines what we see.

16.

Songs of Innocence and of Experience, "The Divine Image" from *Innocence,* copy E. Relief etching with white-line etching/engraving, 4½ x 2¾" (11.2 x 7 cm). Etched, printed, and hand-colored 1789, probably retouched c. 1806.

The poem represents, through its intertwined diction, a unity between the human body and the values of the enlightened soul—the physiology of virtue, as it were. The sweeping curves of a giant, flamelike plant weave a complementary visual unity through the poem's letters and pictorial vignettes. Within the vegetation's upper reaches, two children kneel side by side in prayer. The two women who walk or float toward them are the human forms of the "virtues of delight" to whom "all pray in their distress." A resurrection unfolds, like the raising of Lazarus, in the lower right corner following the reference to God's "dwelling" within the human body. Christ, given a halo in this and several other impressions, touches the raised left arm of a figure whose posture recalls Adam's in Michelangelo's Sistine fresco depiction of the moment when the first man is touched by divine intellect. A second figure, similarly disposed but perhaps female and thus Eve, awaits Christ's attentions. Mortal and immortal equally share the "human form divine." In this context, the slender vine wound about the flame plant becomes another image of Christ (compare his words in John 15:1: "I am the true vine").

The Divine Image.

To Mercy Pity Peace and Love,
All pray in their distress;
And to these virtues of delight
Return their thankfulness

For Mercy Pity Peace and Love,
Is God our father dear;
And Mercy Pity Peace and Love,
Is Man his child and care.

For Mercy has a human heart
Pity, a human face:
And Love, the human form divine,
And Peace, the human dress.

Then every man of every clime,
That prays in his distress,
Prays to the human form divine
Love Mercy Pity Peace.

And all must love the human form,
In heathen turk or jew.
Where Mercy, Love & Pity dwell,
There God is dwelling too

17.

Songs of Innocence and of Experience, frontispiece to *Experience*, copy E. Relief etching, 4³/₈ x 2³/₄″
(11 x 7 cm). Etched, color printed, and hand-colored 1794, probably retouched c. 1806.

The frontispiece to *Experience* establishes a contrary companionship with the frontispiece to *Innocence* (Illus. 14). We again meet Blake's persona, the shepherd-piper (or at least a close relation), and the child-muse. The adult's costume has changed slightly—note the different collar—and he no longer has his pipe (because the songs of innocence have ended?). The child has sprouted wings that should permit continued flight; yet he is now held by the adult. If we take this disposition as an indication of assistance rather than restraint, then the motif recalls the legend that St. Christopher carried the Christ child across a river. The sheep continue to graze in their innocence, but both human figures look directly at us, and thus at the world of experience. Viewed as an abstract pattern, both figures' arms and the child's wings form the outline of a caduceus, the staff of a herald. Like the general title page (Illus. 13), the design seems poised at a transitional moment between states of consciousness, preparing us to "hear the voice of the Bard," Blake's spokesman, whom we meet in the "Introduction" poem to experience. The sky, tinted with the red of sunrise or sunset in this and several other impressions, also announces change.

The bower of the *Innocence* frontispiece has been replaced by a more open, and hence less protective, landscape with distant hills. The vine climbing the tree on the right may be ivy, a traditional image of clinging selfishness that contrasts with the marriage emblem of tree and fruitful vine (see commentary on Illus. 2). Unlike the *Innocence* frontispiece, this design does not directly illustrate any of the texts it introduces. Perhaps this disjunction between verbal and visual images is itself part of our introduction to the divisions between child and adult, man and god, and desire and its fulfillment that characterize *Experience.*

18.

Songs of Innocence and of Experience, "The Sick Rose" from *Experience,* copy E. Relief etching,
4³/₈ x 2³/₄" (11.1 x 6.8 cm). Etched, printed, and hand-colored 1794, retouched c. 1806.

The flowers of innocence, such as those pictured in "Infant Joy" (Illus. 3), become subject to disease and decay in experience. As a traditional symbol of love, the rose can be interpreted as a metaphor for men and women caught in the "howling storm" of sexual passion. Once this human context is established, the disease may be venereal, particularly since eighteenth-century physicians thought that an "invisible worm" caused syphilis. The creative pleasures of "Infant Joy" could not be more thoroughly perverted by a world in which desire gives birth only to death. It is as though Thel's worst fears have come true (see commentary on Illus. 4).

Thorny stems encircle the text. Below, the human form of the rose attempts to flee as a phallic worm enters the flower's "bed / Of crimson joy." Two other figures, apparently female, rest in attitudes of despair on the stems above. The trailing gown of the upper woman associates her with the caterpillar just beginning to nibble on a leaf upper left. The processes of nature are everywhere destroying its beauty.

19.

Songs of Innocence and of Experience, "London" from *Experience,* copy E. Relief etching with slight touches of white-line etching/engraving, 4³/₈ x 2³/₄″ (11.1 x 6.9 cm). Etched, color printed, and hand-colored 1794, retouched c. 1806.

The speaker of "London" journeys through the great city and discovers the visible and audible marks of its decay. Social institutions meant to unite the populace have become mental and physical "manacles." The church only blackens those it should help, the state destroys its own soldiers, and marriage has become a channel for venereal disease from harlot to husband to bride to blinded child. The density of meanings and somber power of "London" make it one of the greatest short poems in English.

The design, not related to specific images in the text, offers an almost Dickensian view of city life. A boy helps an old man on crutches through a street, perhaps leading him to the large door in a stone wall. The two figures are illuminated by a shaft of light in an otherwise darkened world. Contrary to the consistently bleak tenor of the text, the illustration would seem to present an act of charity in the midst of woe. On plate 84 of his final illuminated epic, *Jerusalem,* Blake etched the same arrangement of man and boy to illustrate his personification of the city itself: "I see London blind & age-bent begging thro the Streets / Of Babylon, led by a child."

In a separate vignette, a child, perhaps the chimney sweeper of the third stanza, warms his hands at a fire that billows black smoke. To this image of meager comfort Blake adds the worm of mortality undulating over the earth below the text.

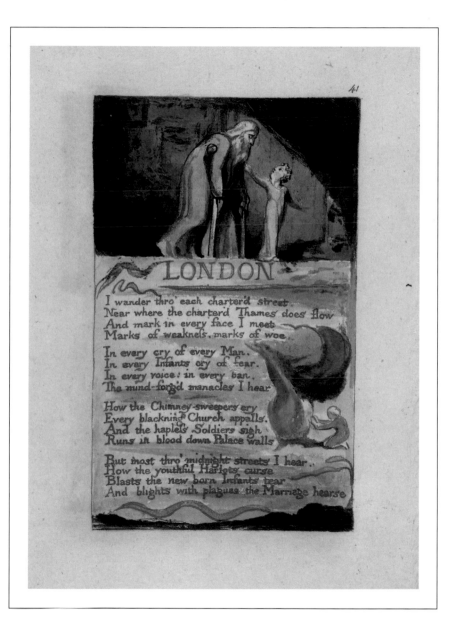

20.

Songs of Experience, "The Tyger," copy N. Relief etching, 4⅜ x 2½" (11 x 6.3 cm). Etched 1794, printed and hand-colored 1795. Call no. 54038

Blake's best-known poem is less about the tiger than the mind of the speaker. He reifies his own fearful vision into the beast and then takes this projection as objective evidence for the nature of the creator, conveniently forgetting that the creator is himself. The result of this compelling but solipsistic exercise is a tigerish universe shaped by a tigerish god. By tracing this psychology of sublime terror, Blake has also written a critique of the chief document on that emotion as an aesthetic mode, Edmund Burke's *Philosophical Enquiry into . . . the Sublime and Beautiful* (1756). Since Burke was also England's greatest critic of the French Revolution and what it represented, "The Tyger" is not without political implications. Blake may be saying, in a veiled way, that the reactionary forces are every bit as violent as revolutionary energies.

Several Blake scholars have remarked on the disparity between the power of the text and the tame pussycat pictured below it. In this and several other impressions, the tiger even seems to be smiling pleasantly. As a visual comment on the text, the design underscores the ways in which the nature of the beast is indeed in the eye of the beholder. It is certainly possible, however, that Blake simply was not capable of etching in relief a more frightening animal on such a small scale. The sky backing the text in this Huntington copy, with its layers of rose, blue, and yellow, seems more decorative than naturalistic.

21.

Songs of Experience, "Infant Sorrow," copy N. Relief etching with touches of white-line etching/engraving,
4⅜ x 2¾" (11.1 x 7 cm). Etched 1794, printed and hand-colored 1795.

In the frontispiece to *Innocence* (Illus. 14), the shepherd-piper sees a child "on a cloud" ("Introduction"

to *Innocence*). In *Experience,* we find instead "a fiend hid in a cloud." The infant of sorrow is as energetic as

the child of innocence, but the same gestures now indicate struggle, not joy. The mother's outstretched

arms may express concern for the babe, but everything else in his world is burdened with constraint: the

woman's heavy gown and capped hair, the bedding, the patterned carpet, and the background bed curtains

that seem to hang from the text and block out the pastoral green of innocence. The fact that Blake's father

and older brother were in the hosiery trade may lie behind the overbearing cloth imagery, epitomized ver-

bally by the "swadling bands" in the text. The intertwined vines of *Innocence* have been replaced by

wickerwork and, top left, by sinister tendrils just beginning to take on the woven pattern of a spider's web.

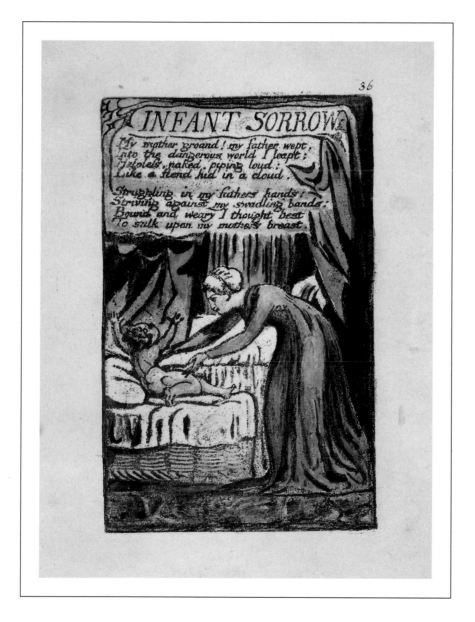

INFANT SORROW

My mother groand! my father wept.
Into the dangerous world I leapt:
Helpless, naked, piping loud:
Like a fiend hid in a cloud.

Struggling in my fathers hands:
Striving against my swadling bands:
Bound and weary I thought best
To sulk upon my mothers breast.

22.

The Song of Los, frontispiece, copy E. Color printed from a copperplate, 9¼ x 6¾″ (23.4 x 17.3 cm).
Designed and printed 1795. Call no. 54043

As the final "Continent" book, The Song of Los continues with the contentions of revolution and oppression, but with even less engagement in immediate political events than America (Illus. 8–10). Blake's central concerns are increasingly with human time on a theological scale, from creation to apocalypse, and with the philosophical underpinnings of mental as well as political tyrannies. America refers to Washington and Franklin, The Song of Los to "Newton & Locke."

The frontispiece shows us the back of a gowned figure bent over an altar bearing one of Urizen's "Books of brass" (plate 7). The worshiper is in thrall to that deity's "abstract Law" (plate 3) and its cosmic representative, a darkened globe that dominates the composition. The mottled forms covering its disc suggest undecipherable hieroglyphics, while its shafts of light form a giant and eerily threatening X.

By the late eighteenth century, astronomers were beginning to speculate about stars with spots revolving on their surfaces and black suns—what we now call black holes. Blake may have been aware of these theories and, if so, used them to imagine an inhuman world of contracted matter that sucks light and life from the universe, the opposite of the human proportions and illumination of Albion rose (Illus. 11). As Blake wrote in his annotations to Emanuel Swedenborg's Divine Love and Divine Wisdom, "the dead Sun is only a phantasy of evil Man."

The graphic technique indicates Blake's evolution toward the planographic printing of his large color prints of 1795 (see commentary on Illus. 26). His printing of intaglio plates, such as Albion rose (Illus. 11), from their surfaces probably showed him that colors could be printed from copperplates bearing at most a scratched outline of the image. The title page and three full-page designs in The Song of Los appear to have been printed in this way, although it is difficult to determine exactly what lies behind the thick color printing. All six extant copies of the book were produced in a single printing in 1795.

23.

The Song of Los, title page, copy E. Color printed from a copperplate, 9⅝ x 6¾" (24.3 x 17.2 cm),

perhaps with scratched outlines for the letters. Designed and printed 1795.

An ancient, bearded man lies on the earth, his form repeating the shapes of the landscape behind him.

His posture resembles engravings of classical river gods, but rather than the traditional vessel spilling life-

giving waters, he holds a skull beneath his left hand. He may be Noah, mentioned on the first text plate

and later described as "white as snow / On the mountains of Ararat" (plate 7). This passage also refers to

Adam as a "mouldering skeleton"; the skull may be his. In spite of these motifs, the scene is not without

ameliorative elements. The composition is more open than the exceptionally oppressive frontispiece

(Illus. 22). Rather than contemplating the skull, as in a traditional memento-mori design, the old man

looks up to the graceful title letters and three birds. The latter recall the dove Noah releases three times to

determine if the waters of the deluge have abated (Genesis 8). The number of birds varies between one and

four in other impressions; in some, the distant peaks suggest waves more than mountains.

24.

The Song of Los, plate 5, copy E. Color printed from a copperplate, 9⅛ x 6⅞" (23.2 x 17.5 cm).
Designed and printed 1795.

A diminutive king (note the crown and scepter) and a sleeping woman, perhaps his queen, rest upon lily blossoms. In this impression he looks to his left with an apprehensive expression. A stream runs through the landscape below and stars decorate the night sky. The frontispiece and final plate of *The Song of Los* (Illus. 22, 25) offer cosmic and geophysical visions, but here we shift to the microscopic and organic. Or are we to imagine that these are giant blooms and the humans of normal size? Such perspectival shifts are central to Blake's thought and the grammar of his art.

The poem's references to the "Kings of Asia" (plate 6) and to a lost paradise and its "joys of Love" (plate 3) may have provided the textual cues for Blake's inclusion of a plate that seems otherwise out of keeping with the tenor of the work. But his reasons may have been intensely personal. The design is based on a wash drawing of two figures resting on a poppy composed by Blake's younger brother, Robert, probably shortly before his death in 1787. Blake kept the notebook containing this drawing all his life and used it extensively himself. Robert's legacy was of particular importance to Blake; as he wrote to William Hayley in 1800, "Thirteen years ago. I lost a brother & with his spirit I converse daily & hourly in the Spirit. & See him in my remembrance in the regions of my Imagination." Blake also executed a watercolor of the design, almost identical to the printed version but reversed, now entitled *Oberon and Titania on a Lily* and dated to c. 1790–93.

25

The Song of Los, plate 8, copy E. Color printed from a copperplate, 9¼ x 6⅞″ (23.5 x 17.5 cm). Designed and printed 1795.

The final plate of *The Song of Los* continues the cosmic perspective of the frontispiece (Illus. 22). Here, however, the spatial relations of the human and the nonhuman are reversed and thus more propitious, with the former now in the superior position. The young man leaning on a hammer is Los, the hero of this "Song" and Blake's embodiment of the artist's imagination, whose name may be "Sol" reversed.

His worried expression is explained by events in *The Book of Urizen:* Los is forced by Urizen's errors into creating, and then inhabiting, the world of fallen time and space. He is resting from his task of forging the suns arrayed around him. Perhaps the largest is our own sun, still partly occluded like the globe on the frontispiece, and the others are stars (known by the late eighteenth century to be solar bodies as well). If we imagine the foreground disc to be rising above the darkness, then we may be witnessing the creation of the living out of the dead sun. The temporality it symbolizes will eventually lead to apocalypse and restoration. In two other impressions, almost the entire surface of the foreground sun is covered with black clouds.

See Illus. 39 for another perspective on Los and the sun.

26

Hecate (or *The Night of Enitharmon's Joy*). Color printed from a millboard or blank copperplate,
16¼ x 22″ (41.5 x 55.9 cm). Designed, printed, and hand-colored 1795. Accession no. 000.126

William Michael Rossetti, who wrote the catalogue of Blake's drawings and paintings for the second volume of Alexander Gilchrist's *Life of Blake* (1863), was the first to call this work *Hecate.* Such a title implies that the female with prominent knees is the classical moon goddess and witch of that name. She is often referred to as "triple Hecate" (for example, near the end of Shakespeare's *A Midsummer Night's Dream*), and thus the young man and woman kneeling behind her are other aspects of her own character. The donkey, owl, lizard, and two bats are Hecate's "familiars," the animals of darkness associated with a witch's evil powers. The book she holds open presumably contains her magic spells. But this title and the subject of the work it implies have been questioned. The nude youths have their heads bent over, as though in shame, and their arms hang limply at their sides as though under a spell—odd images indeed for a witch's own multiple personalities. An alternative interpretation, recently suggested by the art historian Gert Schiff, is that Blake based this design on a speech by the nature goddess Enitharmon in his poem *Europe*:

> *Now comes the night of Enitharmons joy! . . .*
>
> *Go! tell the human race that Womans love is Sin!*
>
> *That an Eternal life awaits the worms of sixty winters*
>
> *In an allegorical abode where existence hath never come:*
>
> *Forbid all Joy, & from her childhood shall the little female*
>
> *Spread nets in every secret path.*
>
> *My weary eyelids draw towards the evening, my bliss is yet but new.*

Enitharmon's "joy" comes from her power to enslave women and men with a combination of sexual guilt and vague promises of an "Eternal life" if her oppressive rules are observed.

There are two other impressions of the print, each showing some variant features. The Huntington's example appears to be the last pulled in a single printing of 1795 in which all three were produced. At some point, probably in the last century, the print was damaged slightly, poorly repaired, and covered with varnish that yellowed over the years. The Huntington had the work cleaned in 1993.

27

Lot and His Daughters. Glue or gum tempera painting with pen drawing, 10¼ x 14¾" (26 x 37.5 cm), c. 1799–1800. Accession no. 000.55

This biblical painting, one of a series Blake painted for Thomas Butts, takes its subject from Genesis 19:30–35. After escaping Sodom and Gomorrah, burning in the distance on the right, Lot finds shelter in a mountain cave. To seduce him into incest, his two daughters make him drink wine, represented by the two cups (one seemingly just dropped by Lot), the wineskin on the right, and the grape vine behind it. Blake pictures Lot asleep as one daughter lifts a cloth from her father's loins, an action not specifically described in the Bible. Halfway between the cave's mouth and the flaming cities is a small, white figure or column— no doubt Lot's wife turned to a pillar of salt (Genesis 19:26). The basic format of the composition and the inclusion of Lot's wife and the cities in the distance follow long-established conventions for this subject; other examples include Peter Paul Rubens's painting, perhaps known to Blake through the 1702 engraving by Jacob Coelmans. Although Blake's version is a straightforward and even traditional illustration to the text, its themes accord with the presentation in his longer poems of the limited physical senses and their subversion at the hands of destructive forms of female sexuality.

As is unfortunately true of almost all of Blake's early temperas, time has not treated *Lot and His Daughters* gently. The medium is inherently unstable and has darkened over the years. The painting has been restored at least once and was at one time framed close to the major figures. This latter attempt to hide damaged areas has left a rectangle of indentations well within the image. In spite of these difficulties, Lot retains his monumentality (reminiscent of the Hercules Farnese) and the daughters their sensuality.

28.

The Conversion of Saul. Watercolor and pen drawing over pencil, 16 x 14″ (40.9 x 35.8 cm), c. 1800. Accession no. 000.29

Saul's dramatic conversion is told in Acts 9:3–7. Christ, surrounded by angels and a suffusion of "light from heaven," directs the man who will become St. Paul toward Damascus. Rather than falling "to the earth," as the Bible describes Saul, Blake pictures him astride a great horse that has gone to ground. Saul looks up to the vision above in rapt awe and extends his arms in a cruciform gesture that foreshadows his acceptance of Christ's crucifixion as a cornerstone of his new faith. One face on the left is turned upward to be illuminated by divine light, but the remainder of the helmeted soldiers accompanying Saul bow their heads and cover their eyes, "hearing a voice, but seeing no man." The single visual witness stresses the corporeality of Christ's presence and suggests that the vision given to Saul can transfigure all but those who willfully turn from the light.

Much remains unknown about the watercolor series of biblical illustrations Blake produced for Thomas Butts. Most of the original mounts have been lost, as is the case with *The Conversion of Saul,* but some of those extant bear the illustrated verses written in a decorative hand. We do not know if the pictures were meant to be hung on the walls of Butts's house or kept in a cabinet or portfolio. Modern scholars have yet to determine if the group is a miscellany based on important passages or if it has some more complex structure embodying Blake's own interpretation of the Bible.

Eight illustrations to John Milton's *Comus.* Pen and watercolor, ranging between 8½ x 7" (21.6 x 17.6 cm) and 8⅞ x 7¼" (22.4 x 18.4 cm). Begun fall 1801 and probably completed no later than 1802.

The *Comus* designs form Blake's first series of illustrations to a work by John Milton, whose poems had so greatly influenced Blake's own. The semicommercial context in which the watercolors were produced, a commission from a specific patron, would have itself inhibited Blake from constructing the sort of radical interpretation of Milton found in *The Marriage of Heaven and Hell* (c. 1790). Yet in spite of Blake's customary fidelity as an illustrator to the text of another poet, we can find subtle differences between Milton's masque, or pastoral entertainment, written in 1634, and Blake's visual retelling. *Comus* valorizes physical virginity in ways that were probably unacceptable to Blake, given his written comments on chastity, and thus he shifts the story toward a psychological investigation of a young girl's sexual fears and fantasies—a theme also central to his own *Book of Thel* (Illus. 4, 5).

In about 1815, Blake painted another series of eight watercolors illustrating *Comus,* now in the Museum of Fine Arts, Boston. These show numerous differences in style and detail from the Huntington set. Milton's poem is cited by line number in the following commentaries.

29. *Comus with His Revelers.* Accession no. 000.20

The design draws on several passages in the poem to introduce the principal antagonists and four different states of organic and spiritual existence—the vegetative, animal, human, and angelic. Comus, a nude youth holding a magician's wand, strides forward in a "Tipsy dance" (104) with men and women he has enchanted and turned into debauched brutes, as indicated by their animal heads (from left to right, a hog, wolf, and lynx). The woman-beast on the left holds aloft a cup that foreshadows its important role in the fifth and sixth designs. By placing Milton's "Lady," as she is called throughout the poem, beneath the revelers, and by giving her a pensive expression, Blake suggests that Comus and his attendants are creatures of her imagination. The roots behind her also seem threatening, but the "attendant Spirit" in the night sky, a "hov'ring Angel girt with golden wings" (214), holds out the promise of protection as the Lady journeys through this "drear Wood" (37). He is not pictured in the Boston version.

30. *Comus, Disguised as a Rustic, Addresses the Lady in the Wood.* Accession no. 000.21

Comus, now in his guise as a "harmless Villager / Whom thrift keeps up about his Country gear" (166–67), approaches the Lady. Like Urizen in Blake's mythological poetry, he is a false father figure. He hides his magic wand (see Illus. 29) behind his back, even though it now plays the role of an old man's gnarled walking stick. It retains the phallic suggestions both it and the revelers' torches have in the first design (Illus. 29). The Lady, here and throughout the series, is never less than modest, but her diaphanous gown reveals her bodily lineaments and adolescent sexuality. Her face and gesture express her confused and unhappy condition, for she is lost in the "rough shades" and "leavy Labyrinth" of the "tall Wood" (266, 270, 278).

Although not present in this scene in the text (244–330), the attendant Spirit has a prominent role in Blake's design. Rays of light emanate from his angelic form. Much later in the masque, the Spirit describes the magical root of "Haemony" (629–47) he gives the Lady's brothers (see Illus. 31) to protect them from Comus's spells. In "another Country," haemony "bore a bright golden flow'r, but not in this soil." A flower, even one specifically described as absent from the "soil" of this world, has an obvious pictorial advantage over an "unsightly root" (629), and thus Blake places a small yellow flower in the Spirit's right hand. Blake has taken a motif named in a later scene and introduced it into an early illustration as an emblem prophetic of the Lady's eventual salvation. Perhaps this flower, like Leutha's in Blake's *Visions of the Daughters of Albion* (Illus. 6, 7), also signifies liberation from sexual anxieties.

31. *The Brothers Seen by Comus Plucking Grapes.* Accession no. 000.22

In his dialogue with the Lady, Comus describes how he came upon her brothers "plucking ripe clusters from the tender shoots" of a "green mantling vine / That crawls along the side of yon small hill" (294–96). The graceful bodies of the youths harmonize with the shapes of the vines, thereby identifying them with the world of nature. They are further associated with innocence by their garb, so similar to the shepherd's in *Songs of Innocence and of Experience* (see Illus. 2, 14). Their vulnerability is stressed by their having left their swords (not pictured in the Boston version) at the foot of the hill. Milton distinguishes between the "elder" and "second" brother, but Blake gives no clear indication of their relative ages anywhere in the series. The Lady compares her brothers to "Narcissus" (237), and there may be something narcissistic, even homoerotic, in their nearly identical lineaments, their rapt gaze at each other, and the intertwined straps of their swords.

Although this scene in the masque is a flashback, Comus is pictured in the villager's costume he does not assume until he addresses the Lady. His expression of feigned humility does not hide malevolent intent. Unlike the brothers, he retains his weapon, the magic rod disguised as a walking stick. In the middle distance are the "labor'd Ox / In his loose traces" and the farmer, even though the latter is described by Comus as sitting "at his Supper" (293). In the background are the tiny figures of the Lady, seated beneath a tree, and the attendant Spirit hovering protectively above. Shafts of radiance illuminate the sky just above the trees; a few jagged pencil strokes above and slightly to the left of the Spirit may indicate the "glancing Star" (80) to which he is compared.

32. *The Brothers Meet the Attendant Spirit in the Wood.* Accession no. 000.23

The attendant Spirit stands in conversation with the Lady's two brothers, all three framed by large trees that make the space between look like the mouth of a cave. He has disguised himself as Thyrsis, their father's shepherd, complete with a satchel and crook. The two gentle youths now hold their swords, if somewhat limply, for they are being armed by the Spirit with knowledge of Comus's evil powers and their sister's peril. The attendant Spirit holds his own weapon, the magical flower of haemony (see Illus. 30).

In his conversation with the brothers, the Spirit refers to the moon goddess "Hecate" (535). This would seem to be the most direct textual prompting for Blake's introduction of the dark and heavily draped figure and serpents in the sky. Another relevant passage is Comus's apostrophe to "Dark veil'd Cotytto" and Hecate, who ride together in a "cloudy Ebon chair" as nocturnal allies in debauchery and sorcery (128–44). Finally, some lines generally not included in *Comus,* but printed in an edition of 1798, refer to a "scalie-harnest dragon" on a "faire tree." This passage may account for the odd way the serpents seem to be perched in the foliage, although Blake's typically flattened perspective may also be a contributing factor. His representation of the serpents, apparently pulling Hecate (or a composite of Hecate/Cotytto) on a flat-bedded vehicle, is indebted to a Roman frieze picturing Ceres on a snake-drawn chariot in pursuit of Proserpine. An engraving of the frieze appears in Bernard de Montfaucon's *Antiquity Explained* (1721), a book Blake almost certainly knew. This source is given iconographic relevance by the identification of Hecate and Cotytto with each other, and with Proserpine, in contemporary handbooks of classical mythology. Further, the story of Proserpine and Ceres centers, like *Comus,* on the struggle between the forces of darkness and of light over a young woman's fate. In the Boston version, a crescent moon hovers in front of the goddess. Blake later used a basically similar arrangement of woman and serpents to personify the moon in his illustrations to the Book of Job.

33. *The Magic Banquet with the Lady Spell-Bound.* Accession no. 000.24

The Lady has been "set in an enchanted Chair" before a table "spread with all dainties" in Comus's "stately Palace" (stage direction following 658). The three large lamps hanging from above may have their textual justification in the Lady's earlier reference to the stars as "Lamps / With everlasting oil" (198–99). Her arms, crossed modestly but perhaps also sensually over her bosom, suggest both her bound physical condition and her attempts to protect the "freedom" of her mind (664). Her peril is underscored by the decorations on the chair—three figures, at least two of whom are female, encircled by serpents.

Comus dominates the scene, as he does the Lady at this juncture in her psychic journey. He holds both his magic rod and a goblet, filled just below the rim with "orient liquor" (65). Five members of his enchanted crew, all with the heads of birds rather than beasts (Illus. 29), stand or sit behind the main adversaries. One of the Lady's brothers refers to a "village cock" (346) in an earlier passage, thereby providing a possible suggestion for the rooster's head below Comus's right elbow, but Milton makes no further references to birds. The portrayal of these avian monstrosities may have been influenced by several pictures of Osiris in Montfaucon's book (see commentary on Illus. 32) and by pictures of sculpted owls in the third volume of James Stuart and Nicholas Revett's *The Antiquities of Athens* (1794), a work for which Blake engraved three plates. The threatening unnaturalness of the banquet is underscored by Comus's rose-purple cape and blue hair, and by the sickly yellow light suffused through the hall. The arches and Doric columns create a classical architectural setting; but it is not certain that Blake is here specifically associating classicism with evil, as he does in his later writings.

In the Boston version, some of the birds' heads are replaced by those of a cat, an elephant, a lion, and a boar. Comus seems to be conjuring up a semitransparent snake from a jar held by a servant. The serpents and human figures decorating the Lady's chair are replaced by shafts of grain, perhaps an emblem of present imprisonment but with the promise of future release.

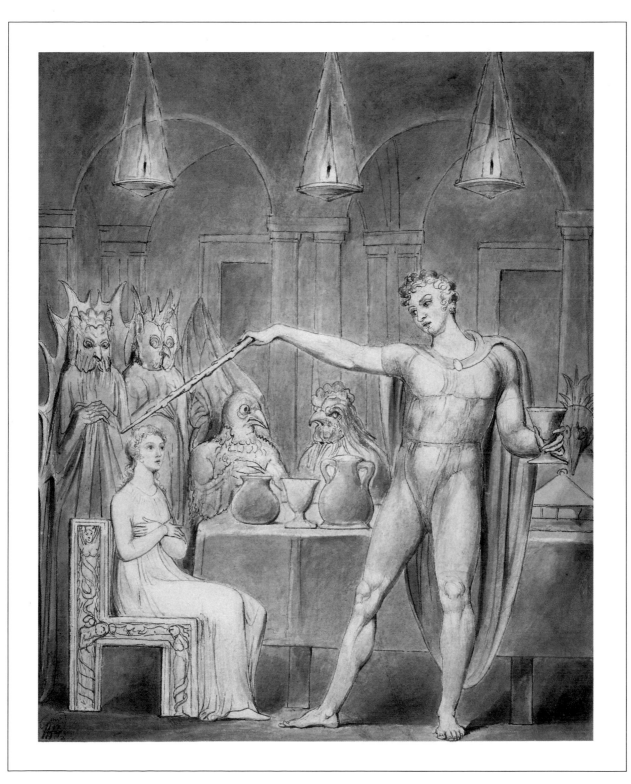

34. *The Brothers Driving out Comus.* Accession no. 000.25

"The Brothers rush in with Swords drawn, wrest [Comus's] Glass out of his hand," and disperse his "rout" (stage direction following 813). The enchanter's palace, for which the lamp just left of the raised swords serves as a visual synecdoche, and the monsters literally go up in smoke to be replaced by two tree trunks and two stars, upper right. Although Milton makes no reference to smoke in this scene, elsewhere he associates it with the dark forest (5) and with those whom Comus has enchanted (655). Comus is nude, as in the first design (Illus. 29), but retains his rod even though the attendant Spirit had instructed the brothers to "seize" it (653). Comus's remaining cohorts are no longer complete figures but only zoomorphic fragments. From bottom to top are the heads of a devil with pointed ears and short horns, a squawking bird, a bearded man with horns, and a horse with nostrils flared. Three batlike wings, similar to those adorning the owl-faced monsters in the fifth design (Illus. 33), are clustered behind. The brothers seem to be looking up at the four heads rather than at Comus. Spellbound and with her hands still covering her breasts, the Lady sits in what appears to be the same rigid chair pictured in the previous illustration. Its sketchy decorations look more like the shafts of grain found in the Boston version of the fifth design than the serpents and figures of Illus. 33.

Much of the smoke seems to be billowing from behind the Lady's chair. This arrangement, considerably altered in the Boston version, suggests that Comus's conjurations are projections of, or at least made possible by, the Lady's own troubled state of mind—a theme first suggested by the opening design (Illus. 29). Thus the dispersal of Comus's band indicates a change in the Lady's psychological condition. But is this an act of liberation from a perverted sexuality or the repression of all libidinal energies?

35. *Sabrina Disenchanting the Lady.* Accession no. 000.26

Sabrina, goddess of the River Severn, "rises, attended by water-Nymphs," to "sprinkle . . . drops . . . from [her] fountain pure" on the Lady to free her from Comus's spell (stage direction following 889 and 911–12). This ceremonious action suggests a baptism. Sabrina's stylish coiffure may have been prompted by the reference to "twisted braids" in the attendant Spirit's song to her (863), although her hair is described as a "loose train" in the next line. She appears to represent Blake's image of adult female sensuality that the Lady has yet to attain. The Spirit, still in his shepherd's garb, points heavenward, a gesture appropriate for his words at the end of this scene: "Come let us haste, the Stars grow high, / But night sits monarch yet in the mid sky" (956–58). Rays of light shooting above the horizon suggest a moment closer to dawn. The Lady's brothers bow toward Sabrina and hold their hands palm-to-palm, as if in prayer. The Lady, seated in the center of the action around her, holds her arms and hands in a gesture hinting at astonishment, but also showing a freedom she lacked in the previous two designs. Yet she remains more acted upon than acting.

As light replaces darkness and as heavenly magic replaces beastly forces, Sabrina's four attendants form a virtuous counterpart to Comus's gang in earlier designs. The nymph far right holds a covered cup or vase, perhaps containing "vial'd liquors" (847), as the positive counterpart to the goblet held by Comus (Illus. 33) and seized by the brothers (Illus. 34). The next woman to the left holds a conch shell and the child left of Sabrina clasps a turbinate shell, possibly a whelk, with both hands. The top of a shell can be seen just above the left shoulder of the remaining nymph. These aquatic creatures, more suggestive of the oceans than a river, were probably suggested to Blake by Milton's reference to "Triton's winding shell" (873). Sabrina and her associates appear to hover a few inches above the gentle waters of the Severn. Only two small girls accompany Sabrina in the Boston version, in which a rainbow arches over all three females.

36. *The Lady Restored to Her Parents.* Accession no. 000.27

The Lady and her brothers have left the dark wood and returned to the home of their aged parents (947 and stage direction following 957). Their humble house on the right contrasts with the malevolent opulence of Comus's palace in Illus. 33. The brothers look to the left and gesture with surprise as they see the attendant Spirit *in propria persona* as a soaring winged figure of uncertain gender (see also Illus. 30). The Lady's mother, wearing a mantle over her head, recalls similar figures elsewhere in Blake's art associated with Vala, the goddess of fallen nature in Blake's mythology, and with other mysterious females like the hooded moon goddess in Illus. 32. The format of the design emphasizes a juxtaposition between the Lady's spiritual guardian on the left and her earthbound parents on the right. The sunrise of a new day breaks over the horizon.

Milton's drama ends in joyous dance and song, as is traditional for a masque. Blake ends his illustrations on a far more serious note, indicated by the facial expressions of all six characters. As a journey toward a spiritual awakening, the designs have led full circle back to the Lady's mortal mother, not to a new mental state that transcends natural consciousness. The attendant Spirit rises and beckons toward a conclusion that the Lady, delivered into the hands of age, will not experience. Further, the Lady's liberation from sexual anxieties has not resulted in sexual maturity but in a return to the childhood condition where she began. Virginity has been preserved, but at the cost of the energy represented by Comus, albeit in a perverted form. What is absent from Milton's poem, as Blake's illustrations emphasize, is a positive form of adult erotic experience of the kind Blake imagines in many of his own writings, or a concept of divine androgyny of the sort found in Blake's later poetry and perhaps hinted at by the sexual ambiguity of the attendant Spirit.

37

Milton a Poem, title page, copy B. White-line etching/engraving, 6¼ x 4½″ (16 x 11.2 cm). Etched c. 1804–10, printed and hand-colored c. 1810–11. Call no. 54041

One of Blake's two conclusive epics, *Milton* follows the great English poet in a journey of self-discovery and renewal. In the first book, Milton returns from heaven to the mortal world and unites with the imagination through the person of William Blake. Together, they set out to reconfigure the relationship between a living poet and a major predecessor. In the second and final book, Milton unites with his feminine aspect (or "emanation," named Ololon) in progress toward the apocalyptic overcoming of divisions between the sexes, between the living and the dead, and between the human and nonhuman worlds. But this plot is almost overwhelmed by Blake's expansive references and allusions that range from the Bible to his own life during the difficult sojourn in Felpham under the patronage of William Hayley (see the Introduction).

Here on the title page, Milton as a muscular nude youth walks into swirling clouds, identified as smoke by the addition of fire in two other copies. At his feet is a paraphrase of the famous line from *Paradise Lost* in which Milton sets out his high ambition. Blake implies that this task is not yet complete and must be taken up again. In the context of the poem's psychodrama, Milton is descending into the vortex of his own being to demolish conventional concepts of the self, much as his hand breaks his name, and to redefine human identity. The heroic figure also represents Blake and his readers, plunging into the dense verbal texture of this poem. By inscribing his words in three directions, Blake disrupts the conventional form of typographic books and requires us to turn the plate in a way that repeats the circular motion of the clouds.

The graphic techniques Blake deployed in the fifty plates of *Milton* are unusual even by his standards. Besides his normal method of relief etching (see the Introduction), Blake made use of two white-line techniques he called "Woodcut [meaning relief] on Pewter" and "Woodcut on Copper" in his Notebook. All three processes are used on copperplates in a bold and rugged manner that creates an antique, even primitive, visual style.

38.

Milton a Poem, plate 15, copy B. Relief etching, 6⅝ x 4⅜" (16.9 x 11 cm). Etched c. 1804–10, printed and hand-colored c. 1810–11.

In a scene presented verbally on plate 17, Milton reaches across the Arnon, a biblical river Blake associates with death, to both sculpt and struggle with Urizen, the creator of the fallen universe and its laws. These Milton must overcome. With his right foot he literally breaks the word "Self- -hood" in the text below to signal the annihilation of his false and deceptive notion of his own identity, a necessary step on his journey toward spiritual and artistic renovation. Urizen, supported by tablets like those of the decalogue given to Moses, seems to be sinking into the waters of death. But Milton must give Urizen external form so that the Urizenic aspects of his own being can be separated from the self and cast out. The Hebrew characters on the tablets do not spell any words, as though the laws Urizen tried to construct have fallen into confusion, just as the universe he created tends toward chaos.

The male and female musicians on the hill above may signify the five liberated senses also announced by the sunrise behind them. But all is not necessarily as it seems in the world of *Milton.* These may be the "sons & daughters" of the false nature goddesses Rahab and Tirzah, who, on plate 17 of the text, "in all their beauty . . . entice Milton across the river" before he has the spiritual strength to overcome the division between life and death.

For another presentation of Urizen as an ancient man, see Illus. 9.

To Annihilate the Self=hood of Deceit & False Forgiveness

Milton a Poem, plate 21, copy B. "Woodcut on Pewter" technique (see Illus. 37 commentary)
used on copper, perhaps with some relief etching, 6¼ x 4⅜" (16 x 11.1 cm).
Etched c. 1804–10, printed and hand-colored c. 1810–11.

This striking image directly illustrates one of the central dramatic events of the poem:

> *. . . I [Blake] bound my sandals*
>
> *On; to walk forward thro' Eternity, Los descended to me:*
>
> *And Los behind me stood; a terrible flaming Sun: just close*
>
> *Behind my back; I turned round in terror, and behold.* (plate 20)

In a letter of 1802 to his patron, Thomas Butts, Blake offers another verbal rendering of the same moment:

> *Then Los appeard in all his power*
>
> *In the Sun he appeard descending before*
>
> *My face in fierce flames in my double sight*
>
> *Twas outward a Sun: inward Los in his might*

Here in *Milton*, the vision unfolds "in the Vale / Of Lambeth," where the Blakes lived in the 1790s, but perhaps we are also meant to see the design from a cosmic perspective that transforms the grassy knoll into the rim of the earth. Los is the spirit of the active imagination, working within the fallen senses and their world but always struggling to expand them. Blake, in the foreground, has a sandal on his right foot; Los, as the poet's muse, will further assist his spiritual journey—that is, the writing of *Milton*. Like Apollo, the god of poetry in classical mythology, Los is associated with the sun—see the final plate of *The Song of Los* (Illus. 25). He appears to Blake as "the angel standing in the sun" appeared to St. John in Revelation 19:17.

The spatial relationship between the figures prompts a contrast with plate 15 (Illus. 38). There Milton attempts to gain power over and to shape the deity above him; here Blake, Milton's successor in the writing of Christian epic, receives from above the power of the shaping imagination. Some interpreters have found in plate 21 a suggestion of oral-genital contact. If this is a valid perspective, then Blake has extended his theme of brotherhood in the poem into an erotic dimension as a powerfully physical embodiment of the union between the artist and the imagination.

40.

Milton a Poem, plate 29, copy B. "Woodcut on Pewter" technique (see Illus. 37 commentary)
used on copper, 6¼ x 4½" (16 x 11.2 cm). Etched c. 1804–10, printed and hand-colored c. 1810–11.

Like plate 21 (Illus. 39), this full-page design shows a crucial moment of union also presented in the

text:

> Then first I [Blake] saw him [Milton] in
>
> the Zenith as a falling star,
>
> Descending perpendicular, swift as the
>
> swallow or swift;
>
> And on my left foot falling on the tarsus,
>
> enterd there;
>
> But from my left foot a black cloud
>
> redounding spread over Europe. (plate 14)

Given the identification of the man and shooting star, the image becomes a striking visualization of the
concept of poetic influence, the process whereby the works of a dead poet enter into and inspire the mind
of a living poet who then continues (yet revises) the voice of his precursor. This may be a night scene, in
accord with Blake's habit of rising late at night to compose his verses when the spirit was upon him. He
falls backward in ecstasy, his arms in a cruciform position recalling Christ's Passion on the Cross. The
design's oddest feature, the descent of Milton into Blake's foot, may be explained by the poem's feet and
journey metaphors for poetic ability and labor. The crude steps behind Blake suggest descent and ascent,
mental as much as physical, as another dimension of this journey. The "black cloud" rising above Blake's
head and between his legs may represent Milton's errors—in Blake's opinion, his Puritanism, rationalism,
and excessive respect for classicism—that must not enter Blake's own consciousness but have unfortunately
spread through the philosophies of Europe.

"WILLIAM" is nude in one copy and wears yellow-green shorts in two others. Here in the Huntington version, only the waistband and cuffs of the shorts were added with a pen. Milton also contains a
mirror-image companion plate. It is inscribed "ROBERT" to identify the figure as Blake's beloved younger
brother, who died in 1787 before his ambitions as an artist could be realized. Biological brotherhood
becomes part of the concept of poetic brotherhood encompassing Milton and the two Blakes.

Milton a Poem, plate 38, copy B. White-line etching, probably with touches of white-line engraving, second state, 5⅜ x 4⅛″ (13.6 x 10.5 cm). Etched c. 1804–10, printed and hand-colored c. 1810–11.

This darkly beautiful composition is made even more haunting by the questions surrounding its meaning. The rocky shore and waves establish an almost primordial setting. The couple's embrace, both loving and erotic, is darkened by the woman's disturbed expression and the man's dangling right arm suggesting fatigue or even death. Is this a pre-, post-, or non-coital scene? Are they threatened by a giant bird of prey, or is this the "Eagle" characterized as "a portion of Genius" in *The Marriage of Heaven and Hell*? Curiously, the closest textual parallel for the design appears not in *Milton* but in Blake's other illuminated epic, *Jerusalem*:

> *Albion cold lays on his Rock: . . .*
>
> *. . . roaring seas dash furious against him*
>
> *. . . England a Female Shadow . . .*
>
> *. . . lays upon his bosom heavy. . . .*
>
> *Over them the famishd Eagle screams on boney Wings. . . .* (plate 94)

Albion, a traditional personification of Britain, plays a significant role in *Milton*, where he is described as lying "upon the Rock of Ages" near "the Sea of Time & Space" (plate 14). These textual contexts further suggest that the woman is Albion's female counterpart, Jerusalem. Their desperate state represents Blake's bleakest vision of our own, one that leaves humanity stranded in an obdurate and menacing world.

The design may also have an autobiographical dimension. In 1802, while living in Felpham near the English Channel, Blake used almost the identical eagle to illustrate a series of ballads written by his patron, William Hayley (see the Introduction). This association suggests that the eagle in *Milton* represents Blake's belief that Hayley was a lesser talent that preyed on his own. If so, then the couple is William and Catherine Blake.

Much critical attention has been given to what appears to be the man's erect penis. The effect is clearest in the British Museum copy but can still be seen in the Huntington's. The motif intensifies the sexuality of the scene, perhaps as a physical metaphor for the moment of inspiration that will transform the couple's lot. But the penis may have been an unintended consequence of Blake's attempt to model the man's belly with fine white lines. In a later and carefully hand-colored impression, the phallus disappears.

Twelve illustrations to John Milton's *Paradise Lost.* Pen and watercolor,
ranging between 9¾ x 8″ (24.8 x 20.2 cm) and 10⅛ x 8⅜ ″ (25.8 x 21.3 cm), 1807.

Blake believed that Milton's two epics, *Paradise Lost* and *Paradise Regained,* were the most important English predecessors to his own epic ventures. Thus, when he was commissioned to illustrate *Paradise Lost,* the task must have seemed a challenge to his abilities as a literary interpreter and an artist. In *The Marriage of Heaven and Hell* (c. 1790), Blake's "Devil" had offered a radical rereading of *Paradise Lost,* which reversed the conventional understanding of the poem and made Satan its hero. Nothing so dramatic unfolds in these illustrations. Even in his choice of subjects—roughly, one for each "Book" of the poem—and composition of some designs (see Illus. 43), Blake tended to follow the established traditions of Milton illustration. In some images, however, we can find associations with Blake's writings that help us perceive his unique perspective on Milton's greatest poem.

This first series of *Paradise Lost* designs was probably commissioned by Joseph Thomas in 1807, the date Blake wrote on some of the watercolors. The group was dispersed in the late nineteenth century but was reassembled by Henry Huntington between 1911 and 1914. Blake also composed a second series of larger images for his chief patron, Thomas Butts. One of these watercolors is also in the Huntington collection—see Illus. 54. *Paradise Lost* is cited by book and line numbers in the following commentaries.

42. *Satan Calling Up His Legions.* Accession no. 000.1

Satan stands above hell's burning lake to rally the other fallen angels to continue their struggle against God (1:299–334). His "baleful eyes" (1:56) and the scales over his genitals (omens of the serpent he will become) signal his fallen condition, but his heroic physique bespeaks residual potency. Satan's "ponderous shield" and "Spear" (1:284, 292) rest on a rock behind and to his left. Some of the damned angels are still chained within the "fiery Deluge" (1:68); others begin to "rouse and bestir themselves" (1:334) in response to their leader's words. Their heavily muscled bodies and contorted postures reveal the influence of Michelangelo's *Last Judgment* fresco in the Sistine Chapel.

43. *Satan, Sin, and Death: Satan Comes to the Gates of Hell.* Accession no. 000.2

Satan, in his flight from hell to earth, enters from the left to be challenged by his incestuous off-spring, Death. Blake has paid close attention to Milton's description of the conflict. The adversaries "frown" and take "horrid strides" toward each other (2:676, 713–14). Satan brandishes the shield and spear pictured at his side in the first watercolor (Illus. 42), while Death, wearing his "kingly Crown," raises his flaming "Dart" with both hands and levels "his deadly aim" at Satan's head (2:672–73, 711–12). The strong diagonals defined by the weapons give linear expression to their conflict and focus attention on Sin, Satan's daughter whom he raped. She rises to separate the combatants. Below her voluptuous torso are the tails of two serpents coiling "in many a scaly fold" and the heads of three "Hell Hounds . . . / With wide *Cerberean* mouths" (2:650, 654–55). These motifs symbolize the combination of seductiveness and destructiveness defining Milton's concept of sin. Her "fatal Key" to "Hell Gate" (2:725) dangles to the right of Death's right calf. Above and behind Satan are two archways, suggesting that he has already passed through two groups of the "thrice threefold" gates and has come to the last set of "Adamantine Rock" (2:645–46). All three figures stand on a plinthlike block of stone.

The basic arrangement of the figures follows the tradition established by William Hogarth. His painting of c. 1735–40 also includes a heavy chain and a "huge Portcullis" (2:874) with vertical bars terminating in points like Death's dart. Hogarth's figure of Death, like most later portrayals influenced by his work, shows him as a skeleton. But Milton describes Death as a "shadow . . . that shape had none" (2:667, 669), and thus Blake indicates Death's insubstantiality by drawing his body in outline but revealing the background through his transparent flesh. Blake thereby remained true to the text without turning away from his characteristic linear style.

See Illus. 54 for Blake's larger version of this design.

44. *Christ Offers to Redeem Man.* Accession no. 000.4

Christ, already assuming a cruciform posture indicative of his destiny, offers to atone for human sins. His open gesture contrasts sharply with the enclosed and static posture of God the Father, "High Thron'd" but "bent Down" (3:58). This pose recalls Blake's many portrayals of the evil demiurge, Urizen (see Illus. 9). The rectilinear, undecorated throne also recalls Urizenic materiality and the hellish stones in the previous two designs. The "Fountain of Light" that makes God "invisible" in the poem (3:375) is reduced to a few rays of light. By hiding the Father's face behind Christ's body, Blake provides a pictorial equivalent of Milton's description of the Son as He through whom "the' Almighty Father shines, / Whom else no Creature can behold" (3:386–87). The energy of the Son is beginning to replace a weakening Father, much as Christ became a significant presence in Blake's later poetry as an antidote to Urizenic forces.

Angels descend on each side of God's throne to "cast / Their Crowns" on the steps before Him (3:349–52). Below, Satan is "Coasting the wall of Heav'n on this side Night / In the dun Air sublime" (3:71–2). His genitals are covered with scales, as in the first design (Illus. 42), and he now holds his shield and spear. Satan's wings, mentioned by Milton for the first time in the passage illustrated (3:73), have disturbingly batlike trailing edges. His saddened visage suggests an awareness that his crimes against humanity will be undone by the actions Christ promises in the scene above. Milton's "wall" at the periphery of heaven has become in Blake's design a parabolic band of clouds, a device he also uses to separate different states of being and consciousness in the fourth and tenth watercolors (Illus. 45, 51).

As in many medieval paintings, this design includes multiple events within a single pictorial space. Satan, "undelighted" (4:286), watches Adam and Eve as they walk side by side in the Garden of Eden. Blake pictures Adam with "Hyacinthine Locks" (4:301) and Eve with the "golden tresses" Milton compares to a vine with curling tendrils (4:305–07). The fallen angel gestures in surprise or consternation, his face "dimm'd" (4:114) and brow knitted as he "falls into many doubts with himself, and many passions, fear, envy, and despair" (Argument to Book 4). Blake captures this sense of self-division (an important theme in his own poetry of this period) and degeneration into a lesser form of being by entwining Satan's winged body with the serpent he will become and by placing the serpent's head in ascendancy over Satan's residually angelic countenance. Bare trees stand beside him, in contrast to the luxuriant foliage and intertwined grape vines, emblems of marriage, behind Adam and Eve. Yet this contrast also establishes a disturbing similarity, for the vines foreshadow the serpent wrapped about the Tree of the Knowledge of Good and Evil (Illus. 47). The mutual self-involvement of Adam and Eve, staring into each other's eyes, adds another warning note. Limited vision, even if an aspect of innocence, is one of the fundamental errors Blake exposes in his writings.

The temporal division between Satan spying on Adam and Eve in Book 4 and the angel Raphael's descent into Eden in Book 5 is given pictorial presence by the V-shaped cloud band surrounding him. Partly "veil'd with his gorgeous wings" (5:250), he intercedes like a spear point between Satan and his intended victims. The seraph looks above to "th' Eternal Father" (5:246) to receive instructions. The gestures, wings, and beard of God are based on a rain god Blake engraved in 1791 after a design by his friend Henry Fuseli as an illustration to Erasmus Darwin's *The Botanic Garden.* As in the previous design, God the Father resembles Blake's portrayals of Urizen in his illuminated books—compare, for example, the evil sky god on the title page to *Visions of the Daughters of Albion* (Illus. 7).

In the series of larger designs, this scene is replaced by *Adam and Eve Asleep* on a bed of flowers with Satan as a toad at her ear (Museum of Fine Arts, Boston).

46. *Satan Watching the Endearments of Adam and Eve.* Accession no. 000.6

The design illustrates the sensuous but innocent moment when Adam kisses Eve while Satan watches with "envy" (4:492–504), but Blake draws on other passages in Book 4 to picture the couple's "happy nuptial League" (4:339). Adam and Eve sit on a "soft downy Bank damaskt with flow'rs" (4:334) over which large sprigs of "Laurel" and roses "without Thorn" (these are prelapsarian roses) form a "blissful Bower" (4:256, 690, 594, 698). The flattened perspective and stylized shapes of the flowers give the scene an other-worldly, even artificial, aura. Eve "half imbracing lean[s] / On our first Father" and looks on Adam "with eyes / Of conjugal attraction unreprov'd" (4:492–95). Her "loose tresses" (4:497) tumble over her right shoulder. Adam wears a wreath of flowers (not mentioned by Milton in this scene) that foreshadows the garland Adam holds during Eve's fall (Illus. 50) and Christ's crown of thorns in the Crucifixion design (Illus. 52).

Satan, poised between the setting sun and the rising moon, glides overhead. The blue coloring of his body, flaccid outlining of his form, and the way one star shines through his upper wing indicate that he is only a ghostly presence, like Death in the second design (Illus. 43). His intertwined rapture with his own serpent form—the "Hell" literally "round about him" wherever he goes (4:20–1)—parodies the scene below. His left hand caresses the snake's head with a gesture very similar to Eve's left hand and Adam's right. Taken together, the two couples repeat the complex analyses of the human self in Blake's illuminated epics, *Milton* (Illus. 37–41) and *Jerusalem.* The bat-winged devil and his serpent roughly parallel the distinction between the self and its "Spectre," an alienated otherness that attempts to dominate the self. Adam and Eve suggest the division of an androgynous humanity into male self and female "Emanation." Here the two are still in a loving embrace that recalls the original unity of the sexes, but this will not last because of the self-divided presence hovering above them and pointing, with the extended index finger of his right hand, to Adam's head.

The archangel Raphael has joined the first couple in their "Bow'r . . . / With flow'rets deck't" (5:375, 379) to answer Adam's questions about creation and deliver God's admonitions against eating fruit from the Tree of the Knowledge of Good and Evil. Raphael's flamelike wings rise to form an ogee arch over his head. With his left hand he points above, probably in reference to the "Almighty" (5:469), and with his right to the prohibited tree in the middle distance. A giant serpent (perhaps not yet amalgamated with Satan) is already wrapped around the tree decorated with thorns to warn against eating its figlike fruit. The animals below include a horse, a Renaissance symbol of lust, who looks back at the tree (perhaps with "Longing," as Satan says, 9:593); an "elephant" (4:345), emblem of concupiscence; a peacock, often associated with pride or vanity but also a traditional sign of immortality; and a "lion" (4:343) who lies down with at least three sheep in this still peaceable kingdom. In the background on the left, "waters fall / Down the slope hills" (4:260–61), to the right of which stands a "stag" (7:469) and another tiny beast. Two large, long-necked birds soar left of the tree; another sits on the topmost branch on the left. This last motif hints at the description of Satan perched "Like a Cormorant" on the Tree of Life (4:194–96).

Adam's gesture, left hand on breast, emphasizes the heartfelt impression Raphael's story is making. Eve leans toward her mate, seemingly more interested in Adam than in the angel—in accord with Milton's (and Blake's?) concepts of feminine subservience: "Hee for God only, shee for God in him" (4:299). In the version of the design in the series of larger watercolors (Museum of Fine Arts, Boston), Eve stands in the center and serves food to both males.

Branches of laurel frame the design on each side. Lilies and roses, miraculously growing on the same vines, complete the upper reaches of the bower. Between the couple and their visitor stands the "Table" fringed with "grassy turf" and laden with "various fruits" in a leafy bowl, a goblet, and a large cup with a delicately twisted handle (5:303–07, 390–91). The seats and table look as though they had been decorated in a proleptic combination of Gothic Revival and Art Nouveau styles.

48. *The Rout of the Rebel Angels.* Accession no. 000.8

Christ, all but His left arm circumscribed by the rim of the sun, bends His great "Bow" (6:713, 763) and aims one of seven arrows at the rebellious angels who are now, at the conclusion of this final battle in heaven, "Hurl'd headlong flaming from th' Ethereal Sky" (1:45). Blake had also pictured a heroically proportioned figure leaning on one knee and reaching down from a great circle in his famous "Ancient of Days," the frontispiece to *Europe* (1794), but there the figure is Urizen in the act of creating and circumscribing the material universe with giant compasses. Here in the *Paradise Lost* illustrations, two groups of three loyal angels hover on either side of the disc of the Son / sun to frame the geometry of spiritual victory. The front-most angel in each group gestures in awe at the spectacle below. Christ's face is taut and "severe" but does not strongly express the "wrath" Milton describes (6:825–26). As in the first design (Illus. 42), the portrayal of the defeated angels shows the influence of the *Last Judgment* fresco by Michelangelo, the artist whom Blake admired above all others. One upside-down head, just left of center, still wears a crown as a reminder of his former status. The central figure just below Christ's arrow may be Satan; the genital scales disfiguring his beauty in the first design are already present. The way several of the damned clutch their heads indicates that the "Wars of Eternity" are "Mental," even if pictured in terms of "Corporeal Strife." Blake makes this distinction between intellectual and physical conflict on plate 31 of *Milton.*

In the version of this design in the series of larger watercolors (Museum of Fine Arts, Boston), Christ's face is milder, perhaps touched by "Divine compassion" (3:141). The faces of the falling angels display stronger expressions of fear and torment.

49. *The Creation of Eve.* Accession no. 000.9

Under the "forming" hand of Christ, Eve rises from Adam's side, her hands together in prayer (8:452–77). Her floating figure recalls Renaissance portrayals of the birth of Venus from the sea. In the poem, Adam relates the event, which he saw "as in a trance . . . / Though sleeping" (8:462–63). These lines provide the textual cue for Adam's almost deathlike sleep and the misty, crepuscular light surrounding Eve and Christ. The moon, the traditional celestial representative of the feminine principle within nature, rises above Eve. Appropriately, this is a new moon, as indicated by its crescent shape pointing to the right (east).

In Adam's recounting of this scene, he does not specifically refer to Christ's presence. Yet Milton consistently attributes the creation of the world to Christ as the Father's "effectual might" (3:170) and the performative incarnation of His creative "Word" (7:163). Thus, Blake's presentation of Christ as Eve's creator does not violate the text even though it stands outside the tradition, established by Renaissance paintings such as Michelangelo's Sistine fresco, that God the Father is the divine creator of Eve. Here and elsewhere throughout the *Paradise Lost* watercolors, Blake takes every opportunity to emphasize Christ's energetic presence. We find a similar emphasis in Blake's late revisions to his long manuscript poem, *The Four Zoas,* probably written shortly before illustrating *Paradise Lost.*

Beginning in *The Book of Urizen* of 1794, Blake treated the creation of the first female as a fall from divine androgyny into division (see also commentary on Illus. 46). In this context, Adam's sleep on a gigantic leaf that extends under Christ can be interpreted as a decline into a lesser, vegetative state of consciousness. In his later writings, however, Blake presents this primal scene as a fortunate fall. As he writes on plate 42 of his conclusive epic, *Jerusalem,* "when Man sleeps in Beulah [a version of Eden], the Saviour in mercy takes / Contractions Limit [Adam], and of the Limit he forms Woman: That / Himself may in process of time be born Man to redeem." By creating Eve, Christ prepares for His own incarnation in her descendant, the man Jesus.

50. *The Temptation and Fall of Eve.* Accession no. 000.10

Blake pictures both Eve's fall and Adam's sudden consciousness of the profound disturbance in Eden caused by that fall. She stands before the thorny Tree of the Knowledge of Good and Evil, first pictured in the background in Illus. 47, and eats of its fruit (9:780–84). Blake closely follows Milton's description of the serpent, balanced on a

> *Circular base of rising folds,* . . .
>
> *Fold above fold a surging Maze, his Head*
>
> *Crested aloft, and Carbuncle his Eyes;*
>
> *With burnisht Neck of verdant Gold, erect*
>
> *Amidst his circling Spires,* . . .   (9:498–502)

Entwining the serpent around Eve's body is Blake's addition to the scene, one that recalls Satan's serpent-bound form in Illus. 45 and 46. One coil covers her loins in anticipation of the shame she will soon begin to feel. In the poem, Eve plucks the fruit directly from the tree, but Blake shows her accepting it from the serpent's mouth in a satanic parody of the innocent kiss in the fifth design (Illus. 46). Her hand, gently cradling the serpent's head as it had previously caressed Adam's, contributes to the erotic implications of this unholy union of woman and beast. The tree is "Loaden with fruit of fairest colors mixt, / Ruddy and Gold" (9:577–78). Its leaves, shaped like an oak's, remind us of Blake's habit in his poetry of associating oak groves with the human sacrifices of the ancient Druids. The roots, covering the ground like tentacles, contribute to the sense of entrapment and repeat in their jagged outline the lightning streaking through the stormy sky. Milton does not describe atmospheric disturbances until Adam's fall (9:1002), but the dark clouds, roots, and lightning offer visual correlatives to the statement, in the main passage illustrated, that "Earth felt the wound, and Nature from her seat / Sighing through all her Works gave signs of woe" (9:782–83).

Adam and Eve had parted shortly before her fall. He stands in the middle distance—although perhaps we are to think of him as being much farther from the tree than Blake's flattened perspective allows—and holds the "Garland" he had been making for Eve's "Tresses" (9:840–41). His gesture of surprise and startled visage show that "hee the falt'ring measure felt" (9:846). His own fall will come soon after.

51. *The Judgment of Adam and Eve: "So Judged He Man."* Accession no. 000.11

Christ, a haloed "mild Judge and Intercessor both" (10:96), stands between Adam and Eve and gestures toward each as He delivers His judgment on them and the serpent (10:163–208). The woman, "with shame nigh overwhelm'd" (10:159), buries her face in her hands, while Adam bows submissively and clasps his hands in prayer. Both have covered their loins with "broad smooth Leaves" (9:1095) of a shape typical of Blake's pictures of oak leaves (from the fatal Tree?—see commentary on Illus. 50). All three figures stand on an enormous, stylized leaf, like the one beneath Adam in Illus. 49, to signal fallen humanity's natural condition of mortality, which even Christ will experience on the Cross. Perhaps the exaggerated creases on His prominently displayed palms also hint at that sacrifice. The serpent, whose penalty is to move on his "Belly groveling" (10:177), undulates just behind and below the raised heels of Adam and Eve, for "Her Seed shall bruise thy [the serpent's] head, thou bruise his heel" (10:181).

Sin and Death, allowed to pass through the Gates of Hell as a consequence of the fall, dominate the top of the design. Their hyperactivity contrasts with the dignified calm of the scene below. They are not present during the judgment scene in Milton's text, and thus Blake has (as in Illus. 45) pictured in one composition two consecutive events. The temporal difference is indicated by the cloud band dividing the design, although its arch may also be the "Bridge" (9:301) Sin and Death have built to earth. The pair seem joined at the waist, as if to literalize Milton's comment that "Death from Sin no power can separate" (10:251). He is recognizably the same figure introduced in Illus. 43, but he is no longer transparent. The fall has given Death substantial being. His darts (a contrastive companion motif to Christ's arrows in Illus. 48) and the liquid emblems of Sin's "Diseases" (11:474) descend below the clouds to indicate humanity's future sufferings. Milton makes no mention of the vials held by Sin, but they have a textual precedent in the apocalyptic narrative of Revelation chapter 16. Her serpentine hellhounds still yap about Sin's middle and Death still wears his crown. Indeed, he reigns over our mortal condition.

52. *Michael Foretells the Crucifixion.* Accession no. 000.12

In his lengthy description of humanity's future, the warrior angel Michael tells of Christ's crucifixion (12:401–35). Wearing a "Helm" like a Roman centurion's and holding his "Spear" (11:245, 249), Michael points and looks toward Christ "nail'd to the Cross" (12:413) below the traditional Latin motto INRI (Jesus of Nazareth, King of the Jews). Christ's heroic proportions and demeanor in previous designs have been reduced to a very human body meant to evoke pity. Adam, no longer wearing leaves around his loins, holds his hands in prayer and gazes up at Christ's face. The cross is raised on a small hill, as is conventional for representations of Calvary. The landscape also accords with the "Hill / Of Paradise" (11:377–78) from which Michael shows Adam this vision of sacrifice and salvation.

The Crucifixion defeats Sin and Death, who now lie at the foot of the cross. Sin's hellhounds, three of whose heads lie on her torso, have also been stilled forever. The upside-down cruciform posture of Sin and Death, foreshadowed by the bearded devil in the first design (Illus. 42), indicates that they are "with him [Christ] there crucifi'd" (12:417). The serpent coils just above the fallen pair, his head pierced by the nail through Christ's feet. This early Christian motif takes its textual cue from Michael's prophecy that the Crucifixion "Shall bruise the head of Satan" (12:430). Blake uses this same symbolism in his poem of c. 1818, "The Everlasting Gospel": "And thus with wrath he [Christ] did subdue / The Serpent Bulk of Natures dross / till he had naild it to the Cross."

Just as Adam slept while Eve "to life was form'd" (11:369) in Illus. 49, she now sleeps "below while thou [Adam] to foresight wak'st" (11:368). She lies in a shallow depression in the ground almost as if she were buried. This close identification between the female and the earth recalls Blake's presentation of nature goddesses, such as Vala, in his poetry. In that context, the separate female principle of fallen nature must be subdued for the masculine self to achieve spiritual insight. Something similar is hinted at in this pictorial interpretation of *Paradise Lost.*

53. *The Expulsion.* Accession no. 000.13

"In either hand the hast'ning Angel caught / Our ling'ring Parents" and leads them "down the Cliff" from Eden (12:637–39). Michael is dressed much as he is in the previous design, but his plumes now surmount a crown rather than a helmet. This slight change, the absence of his spear, and his saddened visage make him less militant. Adam and Eve are once again clothed with leafy vines, symbols of their fallen condition and shame. "Looking back" (12:641) and up, they see a great coiling form similar to the serpent's folds in earlier designs but now representing the "Sword of God . . . / Fierce as a Comet" (12:633–34) that has guided them out of Eden and will become the "flaming Brand" (12:643) that bars them from returning. At the top are guardian "Cherubim . . . / With dreadful Faces throng'd and fiery Arms" (12:628, 644). Their number may have been determined by an earlier description: " . . . four faces each / Had, like a double *Janus*" (11:128–29). Milton does not mention their mounts, the addition of which suggests the four horsemen of the Apocalypse in Revelation chapter 6. The allusion is authorized by Michael's earlier references to "this world's dissolution" and final judgment (12:459–60).

Neither the lightning bolts nor the serpent, its head raised toward Adam, are named in the passage illustrated. The foreground thistles and thorns are not mentioned in Book 12 but receive a textual precedent from Christ's reference to "Thorns also and Thistles" in his judgment of Adam (10:203). All these motifs recall their presence in earlier designs and, like the many visual cross-references throughout the series, help give it thematic unity. Even the lowliest of these motifs, the thorny branches on the ground, have redemptive significance as a reminder of Christ's crown of thorns.

54.

Satan, Sin, and Death: Satan Comes to the Gates of Hell. Pen and watercolor with gold highlights,

19½ x 15⅞" (49.5 x 40.3 cm), c. 1806. Accession no. 000.3

Satan, Sin, and Death from the series of larger *Paradise Lost* designs differs in several ways from the smaller version, although the basic iconography and relationship to the passage illustrated remain the same (see Illus. 43 and commentary). Satan has his left leg forward and is turned more toward the viewer in this larger version. This posture reveals the scales over his genitals, as in Illus. 42. Death, now without a beard, has his left foot advanced and shows us his back. Sin's scaly coils terminate in serpents' heads similar to the snake's in Illus. 50. Their open mouths and forked tongues recall Milton's image of "a Serpent arm'd / With mortal sting" in the scene illustrated (2:652–53). The head of a fourth hellhound now appears just left of Satan's left knee. The vertical bars of the portcullis on the right no longer terminate in spear points and the figures no longer stand on a raised plinth. Their bodies are fuller, more muscular, and more powerful in their dramatic expressiveness.

Blake signed the large *Satan, Sin, and Death* with a monogram he is not known to have used after 1806. The watercolor was probably painted in that year as an independent composition before the series of twelve smaller designs shown in Illus. 42 through 53. Appreciation of the work may have motivated the creation of both the small watercolors in 1807 and the 1808 commission from Thomas Butts for the group of larger watercolors, to which *Satan, Sin, and Death* was added. A lapse of time may explain the inconsistency of showing Death beardless in this design but with a beard in the tenth and eleventh watercolors in the Butts series. Nor are any of the other images in the Butts group touched with liquefied gold. All twelve of the larger watercolors were dispersed at auction in 1868; nine are now in the Museum of Fine Arts, Boston.

A Title Page for Robert Blair's *The Grave: A Spirit Rising from the Tomb*. Pen and watercolor, 9⅛ x 7⅞" (23.8 x 20 cm), 1806. Accession no. 000.30

When in September 1805 Blake was commissioned by Robert Cromek to illustrate Blair's still-popular "Graveyard" poem, first published in 1743, he prepared a number of drawings that were never published (see the Introduction). This handsome title page is among them. The design is dominated by the large tomb bearing the title inscription and rimmed with tendril and lily decorations that symbolize Christ's resurrection. Seated on each side like sepulchral statues are a matched pair of female figures. The veiled face and bat wings of the woman on the left indicate the death of the body and mourning. She holds a scroll—perhaps a list of the dead. Her companion is equally saddened, with head bent low, but her veil does not cover her face. The large, mothlike wings are traditional attributes of Psyche, taken to be a symbol of the immortal soul in Christianizing interpretations of classical myth (see also Illus. 3). Her triumph over death is indicated by the female personification of the soul rising above the tomb. She leaves behind the winding sheets of death (as did Christ at His resurrection from the tomb) and floats heavenward in a shaft of light breaking through clouds.

The role of this title page, with its 1806 date, within the *Grave* project is difficult to ascertain. Blake may have executed the design in 1805 and dated it in anticipation of publication in the next year. The inscriptions make no mention of Blake being the *engraver* of the designs, as was originally planned, and thus the drawing may have been composed after Blake knew that Cromek had given the graphic execution of the illustrations to Louis Schiavonetti. To promote his forthcoming book, Cromek exhibited some of Blake's drawings in the summer of 1806. Even though his relationship with Cromek was near the breaking point by then, perhaps Blake executed the design as a title page for an advertising portfolio of drawings. The Cromek family owned this drawing until at least 1865. It was acquired by the Huntington in 1924, tucked into a copy of Cromek's 1808 edition of Blair's *Grave*.

A Series of Designs:
Illustrative of
The Grave
a Poem
by Robert Blair.

Invented & Drawn by William Blake.
1806

Six illustrations to John Milton's "On the Morning of Christ's Nativity." Pen and watercolor,
ranging between 6 1/4 x 4 7/8" (15.7 x 12.2 cm) and 6 1/4 x 5" (15.8 x 12.5 cm), c. 1815.

Milton's "Nativity Ode" celebrates, in highly musical verse, the overthrow of classical and other pagan deities at the birth of Christ. Blake first composed a series of six watercolor illustrations for the poem in 1809; these are now in the Whitworth Art Gallery, Manchester, England. A second group of smaller watercolors can be dated to c. 1815 on the basis of their style, characterized by free pen drawing and jewel-like coloring. This set, in the Huntington Art Gallery since 1916, contains what are arguably the most beautiful Blake watercolors in the collection.

As usual, Blake followed the text closely; but the very brevity of the poem, and its many references to figures and events not described in detail, allowed a certain freedom of interpretation. And unlike the *Paradise Lost* designs, those for the "Nativity Ode" had no long illustrative tradition either to assist or inhibit their development. The "Nativity Ode" is cited by line number in the following commentaries.

56. *The Descent of Peace.* Accession no. 000.14

Blake opens the series with a Nativity scene implied by, but not described in, the beginning of the poem. We see the traditional stable as though in cross section, framed by beams in the form of a Gothic archway. The building provides an architectural equivalent of the "House of Mortal Clay" (14), the human body in which Christ is incarnate. Within, the infant Jesus springs into the air with a suffusion of light around His body. To the right is the Virgin, leaning back into Joseph's arms as though swooning with exhaustion or ecstasy. To the left are the young John the Baptist, his mother, St. Elisabeth, and the bearded figure of John's father, Zacharias. Two oxen are behind, their muzzles hidden by what may be hay.

Above the stable, personified "Peace" (46) descends from a tripartite "turning sphere" (48), her arms and each "Turtle wing . . . dividing" (50) the clouds and complementing the triangular roof line. She holds "her myrtle wand" (51) in her right hand. Below the stable is the female form of "Nature" (32). "Innocent Snow" (39) covers the foreground and frosts what is presumably vegetation (trailing over poles?) on each side of the stable.

57. *The Annunciation to the Shepherds.* Accession no. 000.15

The "helmed Cherubim / And . . . Seraphim / Are seen in glittering ranks with wings display'd" (112–14). The former stand in "a Globe of circular light" (110) radiating through the sky and dominating the entire design. The Cherubim raise their arms in an interlaced crossing pattern that Blake used in several of his finest pictures to indicate harmony within a community of the spirit. The circumference of the "Angel Choir" (27) is outlined by the Seraphim, two blowing trumpets (perhaps an omen of the "trump of doom" at the Last Judgment, 156) and several holding timbrels. Below are "the Shepherds on the Lawn / . . . in a rustic row," their gestures expressing the "blissful rapture" with which they greet the announcement of Christ's birth (85–6, 98). The eight foreground figures suggest a family group of men, women, and at least one child. They are accompanied by their "sheep" (91), including a ram on the far right, and two dogs (lower left and left of the second figure from the right). Two, or perhaps three, pyramid-shaped tents indicate the nomadic life of these simple folk. We can see on the distant horizon the stable of the Nativity, now and in its two later appearances (Illus. 58, 61) with lateral extensions on each side of the rectangular building introduced in the first design. The cruciform structure in which Jesus is born foreshadows the cross on which He will be crucified. The tiny outline of a human figure is barely visible inside the stable. In the larger, Whitworth version, we can clearly see Joseph and Mary under the building's Gothic arch.

58. *The Old Dragon.* Accession no. 000.16

The pagan gods are pictured "under ground, / In straiter limits bound" (168–69). Milton later describes their imprisonment in "th' infernal Jail" (233) as occurring when the sun is "in bed" (229). Both the dark tones Blake used to color the design and the rather chaotic arrangement of the underground figures contrast sharply with the radiance and angelic geometry of the previous design. The largest, central demon is "th' old Dragon" (168) who "Swinges the scaly Horror of his folded tail" (172). His seven heads (at least two of which seem female) and the way his tail joins a band of stars indicate that Blake has drawn upon the "great red dragon" whose "tail drew the third part of the stars of heaven" in Revelation 12:3–4. Thus, Blake has returned to one of Milton's own sources of inspiration to flesh out the pictorial imagery. The dragon holds a heavy Roman sword in his left hand and in his right a staff topped by a finial in the shape of a pomegranate, a fruit associated with hell. Snakes twine around the monster's ankles.

Below the old Dragon sits a scaly creature with webbed hands. This is Dagon, referred to in the ode as "that twice-batter'd god of Palestine" (199) and described as half-man, half-fish in Milton's *Paradise Lost* and as a sea monster in Blake's own poem, *Milton.* The woman upper left with a veil or mantle over her head may be "Ashtaroth" (200), another name for the Phoenician moon goddess Astarte. The writhing human bodies, lower right and left, recall the fallen angels in Blake's first and seventh illustrations to *Paradise Lost* (see Illus. 42, 48). Hellish flames rise just below the figure on the right. The company of fallen gods is completed by the bearded face and shadowy body just below ground level on the right.

The stable, a humble reminder of an infant stronger than all the fearsome devils below, anchors the upper, above-ground section of the design. The three figures kneeling before the light-filled center of the building immediately suggest the three wise men, although the events of the poem take place before the arrival of the "Star-led Wizards" (23). Two large angels stand in profile on either side of the Gothic portal, their wings extended over the pitch of the roof. The slight outlines of two standing figures, probably Mary and Joseph, appear within.

59. *The Overthrow of Apollo and the Pagan Gods.* Accession no. 000.17

The asymmetrical composition and its rather cluttered appearance bespeak the disarray that the birth of Christ has brought to paganism. The "parting Genius" (186) of Apollo, his mouth open slightly in a "shriek" (178), dives down in an arc of pale flames and leaves behind his now spiritless statue (173–78). The sculpture is a reasonably accurate representation of a cast of the Apollo Belvedere in London's Royal Academy, engraved by Blake in 1815 for an encyclopedia article, but with the bow added and the python around the tree stump enlarged. Below the statue is an altar in the shape of an Ionic column. Its flames point downward, as though the sacrificial fires are now becoming hellish and destructive. At the base are four worshipers, perhaps "Flamens" (194) and/or the "Tyrian Maids" who, bowing in prayer and "lament" (183), "their wounded Thammuz mourn" (204). A woman on the right wails within a confining cavern in the "steep of Delphos" (178) rising in the background. She is probably one of the "Nymphs" who "in twilight shade of tangled thickets mourn" (188) the overthrow of her god. The small trees on the hill to the left of her represent the "poplar pale" (185) and the thicket of the Nymphs.

On the top of Delphos and in front of a classical colonnade are a band of ill-defined ink lines and washes that suggest departing spirits, as in the more clearly drawn Whitworth version. Two forms at the top have bat wings—always a sign of the deadly or Satanic in Blake's art (compare Illus. 44, 55). Between the colonnade lower left and the descending Genius, a ghostly figure hovers above the sea, probably a visualization of "a voice of weeping heard" over "the resounding shore" (182–83).

In the last two decades of his life, Blake developed a complex critique of classical civilization. He believed that many of its great artifacts preserved the forms of more ancient, Hebraic art, but that the spiritual meanings of these original images had been distorted by the Greeks, Romans, and contemporary classicists for their self-serving purposes. Given these views, Milton's ode on the destruction of the pagan gods provided Blake an opportunity both to display his knowledge of classical sculpture and to indicate the superiority of his own Hebraic and Christian worldview.

60. *The Flight of Moloch.* Accession no. 000.18

The center of the composition is dominated by the "burning Idol all of blackest hue" of "sullen Moloch" (205, 207). The Canaanite and Phoenician devil-god, his bat wings extended, flies away in dark smoke above the crowned and sceptered idol, much as the Genius of Apollo departed his statue in the previous design. Below the idol is his "Ark" (220) in the form of a furnace raised slightly on a circular plinth, with its arched mouth just below the giant's right foot. Two similarly arched mouths or vents also belch flames from the ends of the transverse extensions. This cruciform structure, more clearly defined in the earlier Whitworth version, mimics its spiritual opposite—the stable of the Nativity as pictured in Illus. 57, 58, and 61. The fires of the furnace reach upward toward the idol. The pagan god is being consumed by the fiery sacrifices that had nourished it.

Bearded men on the left and youthful females on the right "dance about the furnace" (210) below the idol. These worshipers and the timbrels in their raised hands are fallen parodies of the chorus of angels who announce Christ's coming in Illus. 57. Here again, Blake presents the pagan as a perverse variant on Hebraic and Christian traditions.

In *Paradise Lost,* Milton describes the child sacrifices practiced by the followers of Moloch. These rites are not described in the "Nativity Ode," but this would seem to be the activity Blake pictures in the lower part of the composition. Two children reach toward the idol just below his right foreleg; a third dangles limply from his left hand. The saddened man and woman in the foreground have apparently cast their child into the fiery maw. But this babe strides miraculously out of the flames in an energetic posture recalling Jesus in the first design (Illus. 56). As with the triumph of Christ over paganism, this innocent child is more powerful than the forces of evil now literally going up in flames.

61. *The Night of Peace.* Accession no. 000.19

Milton and Blake return us to the "Courtly Stable" (243) where we began. The gray and dark blue coloring of the design and the closed eyes of the Holy Family indicate that this is a night scene. The "Virgin . . . / Hath laid her Babe to rest" (237–38). He is now "sleeping" (242) on a bed of straw, perhaps placed on the manger clearly pictured in the Whitworth version. His mother also rests on straw and leans her head toward her child in mutual support within a shared aura of light. Joseph, with a mantle and small halo over his head, stands behind. At each side of the portal is a guardian angel, "helmed" like the Cherubim in Illus. 57 but also "sworded" like Milton's Seraphim (112–13). They "sit in order serviceable" (244) on what appears to be a cloud, or perhaps snow, curving below the stable. Just behind are the two angels introduced in Illus. 58, with their large wings extended along the roof, but now holding spears. Four more spears indicate the presence of additional heavenly protectors. Two angels, "harping in loud and solemn choir" (115), float symmetrically in the sky above the roof line of the stable's transverse wings. In the niche formed by the angels' bodies and wings is a personification of "heav'n's youngest-teemed Star," the star of Bethlehem, sitting in "her polisht Car" (240–41). Her resting steeds and chariot are supported by a bed of clouds. She holds a "Handmaid Lamp" (242) with rays of light forming a starlike pattern around it.

The arches of the stable's entrance provide a final Gothic note to the "Nativity Ode" illustrations. This style is the aesthetic and spiritual contrary of the classical and pagan sculpture also represented in the series. As Blake wrote in *On Homers Poetry* [and] *On Virgil,* "Grecian is Mathematic Form[;] Gothic is Living Form," just as Christ is the living form of God's word. But the design also hints at forces that can smother these beneficent incarnations. The sleep of Jesus and the military angels suggest His passage into the fallen world. For Blake, the worldly church militant distorted Christ's message just as surely as classical civilization had perverted the spiritual vision it had inherited.

Old Parr When Young. Pencil sketch, 12 x 7 ¼" (29.7 x 18.4 cm), 1820. Accession no. 000.48

Blake's new patron and fellow artist John Linnell introduced him to the landscape painter John Varley in 1819. By the fall of that year, Blake began to draw, at Varley's behest, portraits of various historical and imaginary personages Blake would call up before his mind's eye. During these séance-like sessions, he produced over a hundred pencil drawings, now called the "Visionary Heads." Varley seems to have believed literally in these supposed apparitions; Blake probably considered them to be projections of the imagination. Nine of these drawings are in the Huntington Art Gallery. *Old Parr When Young* is the finest in the collection, and one of the few that shows the entire body.

Thomas Parr (or "Par") died on November 15, 1635, reportedly at the age of 152 years 9 months. Blake may have learned of this legendary figure from John Taylor's popular essay and poem, *The Old, Old, Very Old Man: or, The Age and Long Life of Thomas Par.* Blake's portrayal is not based on a likeness of the man, but on his own concepts of the heroic male nude. The thick musculature, but not the stance, recalls the Hercules Farnese, a copy of which Blake had engraved in 1816 to illustrate an encyclopedia. The sketch also corresponds to Blake's idealization of the "Strong Man," one of the "three general classes of men" Blake pictured in his now-lost painting *The Ancient Britons* and discussed in his *Descriptive Catalogue* of 1809. Parr would seem to epitomize Blake's characterization of the Britons of old as "naked civilized men" and the "strong Man as a receptacle of Wisdom, a sublime energizer." His power is expressed in his "compactness, not extent nor bulk," and he acts "from conscious superiority, and marches on in fearless dependance on the divine decrees, raging with the inspirations of the prophetic mind." These comments suggest that Parr's impressive physical presence is the outward expression of a mental state, the inspired or "prophetic mind," in which Blake himself participated in the imaginative act of drawing the "Visionary Heads." As a visual metaphor for that which transcends nature, "Old Parr" bears comparison with Blake's other great male nude, *Albion rose* (Illus. 11).

Varley wrote the inscriptions at the bottom of the drawing. These read "old Parr when young Viz [age] 40" and "Aug 1820– W. Blake. fect.," meaning that Blake made the drawing in August 1820.

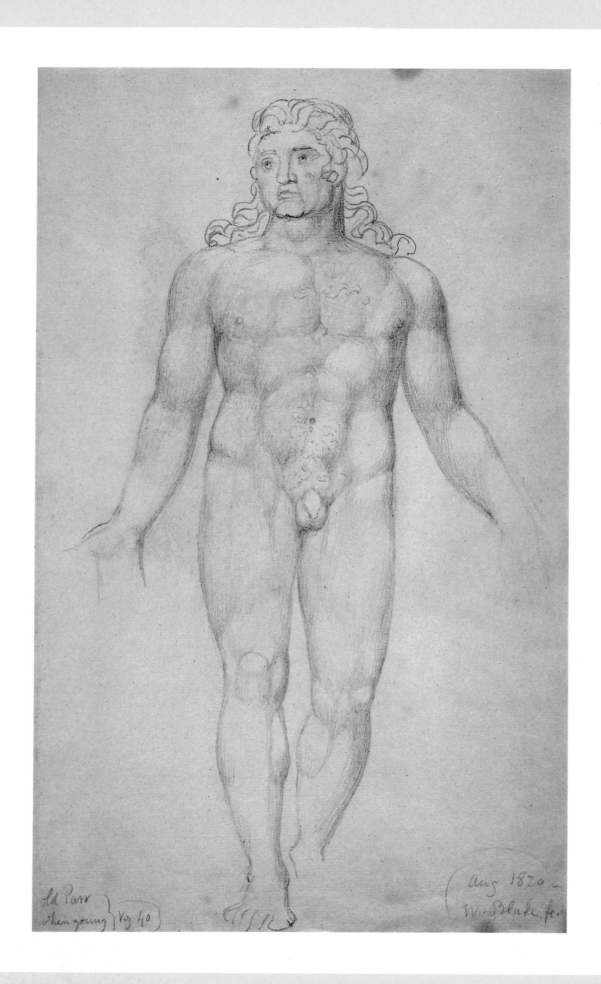

Old Parr
when young Vg 40

Aug 1820 —
W. Blake fe.

63.

Moses Placed in the Ark of the Bulrushes. Pen and watercolor over pencil, 11¼ x 15⅝″ (28.6 x 39.7 cm),

c. 1824–26. Accession no. 000.28

Jochebed, Moses' mother, has already placed the infant in "an ark of bulrushes, . . . and laid it in the flags by the river's brink" (Exodus 2:3). She sinks against her husband, Amram, in weariness and concern for the child's fate. The couple's disposition echoes the presentation of Joseph and Mary in Blake's first design for Milton's "Nativity Ode" (Illus. 56), a similarity suggesting that this event in the life of Moses foreshadows Christ's coming. The large palm near the right margin, a traditional emblem of resilience, may also have a prophetic dimension as a reference to Christ's entry into Jerusalem. Moses' sister, Miriam, stands like a statue on the wall extending into the Nile, "to wit what would be done to him" (Exodus 2:4).

In Blake's mythological poetry, Egypt is cast as a place of slavery and its culture a fallen and perverted form of rational materialism. This context suggests that the watercolor's sphinx, distant pyramids, and what may be brick kilns on the river's far bank have sinister implications. Moses, as the embodiment of the prophetic spirit, has descended into a world badly in need of his vision. The saddened faces of his parents embody fears for his survival in a contest between godly and pagan forces—again as in Blake's "Nativity Ode" illustrations.

Blake was commissioned in 1824 to design and engrave a small illustration of the "Hiding of Moses" for an annual, titled *Remember Me!*, by the book's editor, R. J. Thornton. The published plate and the watercolor are the same design with differences only in details and the extent of the image shown on the left. Even though it is many times larger than the engraving, the watercolor may have been prepared as a preliminary design. It seems more probable, however, that the drawing was begun as an independent composition, perhaps a year or two later than 1824. Blake never finished coloring the work, for Moses and his ark are only sketched in pencil.

A Title Page for an Illustrated Manuscript of Genesis. Pencil, pen, and watercolor with gold highlights,
13⅜ x 9⅜" (34.1 x 23.9 cm), c. 1826–27. Accession no. 000.33

Near the end of Blake's life, John Linnell commissioned him to create an illuminated manuscript of
Genesis. Blake left this work unfinished at his death in August 1827, having written out the text through
Genesis 4:15 on eleven leaves, all now in the Huntington collection. None of the illustrations were
completed; only two variant title pages bear more than touches of watercolor. What is presumably the first
version has the same basic format as the second, reproduced here, but is less finished.

Four major figures are arranged symmetrically around the decorated title letters. The bearded man in
a mandorla on the right is God the Father. The wavy black lines (blue in the first version) above and below
Him indicate that He is dividing the waters (Genesis 1:7). The energetic figure at the top is the Holy
Ghost, his giant wings recalling the dove traditionally used to represent Him. On the left is the Son who,
with His extended left hand, is giving a scroll to Adam, the lowest figure in the group. Given Christ's cruciform posture, this scroll may be a written covenant of man's eventual salvation. The capital "I" does double
duty as a loincloth for Adam, whose new divinity is signaled by a halo. All the title letters spring into vegetative life, including lotus, wheat, lilies, and roses.

Adam stands like a colossus on the rim of the earth. Below are the Trees of Good and Evil and of
Life and four men with the heads of an ox, a lion, a bird, and a reptile. These heads recall three of the
Evangelists: the lion, eagle, and ox of St. Mark, St. John, and St. Luke. Perhaps the reptile is Blake's own
invented symbol for the final Evangelist, St. Matthew, not traditionally identified with any beast. Two further biblical groups are evoked by Blake's figures: the vision of the four faces in Ezekiel 1:10 (man, lion, ox,
eagle), and the four creatures, called "zoa" in the original Greek, of Revelation 4:7 (lion, calf, man, eagle).
This final gathering connects the Genesis title page with Blake's own "Zoas," the four basic constituents of
cosmic and psychic being in his mythological poetry.

A complete, scholarly catalogue of the Huntington's Blake collection—including letters, annotated copies of books from Blake's library, and commercial engravings not noted in this volume—is available in Robert N. Essick, *The Works of William Blake in the Huntington Library* (1985). The standard bibliography of Blake's writings and of books containing his engravings is G. E. Bentley, Jr., *Blake Books* (1977, supplement forthcoming). The authoritative catalogues of Blake's work as an artist, all generously illustrated, are Martin Butlin, *The Paintings and Drawings of William Blake,* 2 vols. (1981); Essick, *The Separate Plates of William Blake* (1983); and Essick, *William Blake's Commercial Book Illustrations* (1991). All the prints both designed and executed by Blake are reproduced in David Bindman, *The Complete Graphic Works of William Blake* (1978).

The two most widely read and quoted editions of Blake's writings are Geoffrey Keynes, ed., *The Complete Writings of William Blake* (1957, frequently reprinted), and David V. Erdman, ed., *The Complete Poetry and Prose of William Blake* (revised edition, 1982). Keynes added normalized punctuation to his texts. Erdman, whose edition is quoted in this volume, prints Blake's idiosyncratic punctuation with some alterations based on context. Between 1951 and 1976, the Blake Trust, in association with the Trianon Press, issued a series of collotype and hand-painted facsimiles of the illuminated books with exceptional fidelity to the originals. In the last few years, the Trust has sponsored the publication of *William Blake's Illuminated Books.* This five-volume series contains complete color reproductions accompanied by letterpress texts, introductions, and helpful annotations. *The Illuminated Blake* (1974), annotated by Erdman, provides black-and-white reproductions of all the illuminated books.

Alexander Gilchrist's *Life of William Blake,* first published in 1863, is one of the classics of British biography. Mona Wilson, *The Life of William Blake* (1927), is also useful. All extant documents about Blake's life are reprinted, and woven into a very readable narrative, in Bentley's *Blake Records* (1969, supplement 1988).

Books on Blake's ideas and writings abound, with more published each year. For those with a serious interest in the subject, a good place to start is with the classic studies that have been most influential: S. Foster Damon, *William Blake: His Philosophy and Symbols* (1924; see also Damon's *A Blake Dictionary,* 1965); Northrop Frye, *Fearful Symmetry: A Study of William Blake* (1947); Erdman, *Blake: Prophet Against Empire* (1954);

and Morton D. Paley, *Energy and the Imagination: A Study of the Development of Blake's Thought* (1970). More recent studies, responsive to contemporary critical perspectives, include Nelson Hilton, *Literal Imagination: Blake's Vision of Words* (1983); Essick, *William Blake and the Language of Adam* (1989); and Vincent Arthur De Luca, *Words of Eternity: Blake and the Poetics of the Sublime* (1991).

The standard art-historical study of Blake is Bindman, *Blake as an Artist* (1977). The relationships between Blake's words and pictures are explored in Jean H. Hagstrum, *William Blake Poet and Painter* (1964), and W. J. T. Mitchell, *Blake's Composite Art: A Study of the Illuminated Poetry* (1978). Blake's aesthetic concepts are set forth and analyzed in Morris Eaves, *William Blake's Theory of Art* (1982); see also Eaves's *The Counter-Arts Conspiracy: Art and Industry in the Age of Blake* (1992). For the full range of Blake's work as an engraver and etcher, see Essick, *William Blake Printmaker* (1980). Joseph Viscomi's *Blake and the Idea of the Book* (1993) presents a wealth of new information on the production history of the illuminated books.

The journal-of-record for Blake scholars is *Blake: An Illustrated Quarterly,* edited by Eaves and Paley and published at the University of Rochester. It includes annual checklists of publications related to Blake and of sales of original works by Blake and his circle.

INDEX

Page numbers in *italics* refer to illustrations.